CONSTRUCTIVE CHANGE IN LATIN AMERICA

CONTRIBUTORS

Germán Arciniegas

Dwight S. Brothers

Fernando H. Cardoso

John P. Gillin

James M. Malloy

John P. Powelson

José Luis Reyna

Richard S. Thorn

CONSTRUCTIVE CHANGE IN LATIN AMERICA

EDITED BY COLE BLASIER

UNIVERSITY OF PITTSBURGH PRESS

To the memory of
EDSEL B. FORD

Preface

Constructive Change in *Latin America* is one of the byproducts of the first in a series of Faculty Seminars on Latin America introduced at the University of Pittsburgh in late 1965. The primary purpose of these seminars was to strengthen the Latin American component of the University's international programs. The seminars provided a meeting ground for scholars from different disciplines, most of whom were recently appointed to the faculty, and helped stimulate the interdisciplinary links vital to teaching and research. Faculty from a dozen or more departments participated. About half of the contributors, Professors Gillin, Malloy, and Thorn, are members of the Pittsburgh faculty, and Professor Powelson taught at Pittsburgh in 1965 and 1966.

All of the essays are concerned with Latin America's growth and development. Although the authors draw on much historical ma-

terial, each treats his subject in terms of his concern for the present
and the future. Participants were encouraged to deal with topics having policy implications. Although the theme of the book is general
and deals with Latin America as a whole, the collection makes no
claim to comprehensiveness. Two of the contributors confined their
studies largely to single countries. John Gillin's observations are
based largely on his experience in a Guatemalan village, and James
Malloy analyzes the interaction of revolution and development in
Bolivia. The other contributors deal with some specific problems
pertinent to the development of Latin America as a whole.

Constructive Change in Latin America is dedicated to the memory of Edsel B. Ford partly because the Ford Foundation, which his
father and he established in Detroit in 1936, provided funds for the
Faculty Seminars. Through a grant for international training and
research the Foundation gave financial impetus to the University of
Pittsburgh's Center for Latin American Studies.

There is another, personal reason for dedicating this book to
Edsel B. Ford. Grown men seldom have heroes, but high school
boys do. As a student in the school of whose board of trustees Mr.
Ford was chairman, I admired him for qualities that are not always
found in men who inherit or earn great wealth. His invariably polite,
self-effacing, and considerate manner reflected concern for others
and a deep sense of civic responsibility. In the rough and ready
circle of Detroit's industrial giants in the mid-1930's no one was
more respected for taste, judgment, and compassion.

The significance of Edsel Ford's influence was far greater than
that of most corporate presidents because of the crucial role the
Ford Motor Company and the Ford fortune played in the resolution
of major issues in the development of American life. As published
memoirs have since revealed, Edsel Ford's foresight, persistence,
and courage led the Ford Motor Company in its retreat from a
policy of rugged individualism to the more enlightened and socially
viable position of today.

Bonnie Wilds and Derk Piel S. translated the Arciniegas and Cardoso-Reyna essays, respectively. The secretarial assistance of Mrs. María Toner is also gratefully acknowledged.

COLE BLASIER

Contents

List of Tables

Introduction

Tһ е contributors to this volume are widely spaced on the spectrum of Latin American scholarship. Some are senior scholars, others younger men; five disciplines are represented; and the authors come from Brazil, Spanish America, and the United States.

Germán Arciniegas and John P. Gillin are from that older generation which was instrumental in introducing Latin America to readers in this country several decades ago. Under the sponsorship of his publisher, Alfred A. Knopf, Mr. Arciniegas brought some of Latin America's best fiction and essays to the attention of North American readers. Mr. Gillin wrote pioneering studies of village communities in Peru and Guatemala based on extensive field work. Two other contributors, Fernando Cardoso and James Malloy, still in their early thirties, bear the stamp of a totally different tradition. While Germán Arciniegas and John Gillin rely heavily on personal observation and intuition nurtured by their long experience, Mr. Cardoso's and, to a lesser extent, Mr. Malloy's conclusions are tied more closely to quantifiable data. Arciniegas' elegant and richly textured prose is in the tradition of the nineteenth century *pensadores*. Gillin's simplicity and clarity of style were developed in an era when Latin Americanists were reaching out for public recognition and support. Cardoso and Malloy, although not economists, show the influence of training in a period when attention has been focused on economic development. Their approach reflects greater preoccupation with theory, methodology, and "science."

Constructive Change in Latin America is an attempt to focus the skills and insights of scholars from five disciplines on the central problem of the region's growth and development: anthropology (Gillin), economics (Brothers, Thorn, and Powelson), literature (Arciniegas), political science (Malloy), and sociology (Cardoso and Reyna). Multi-disciplinary approaches like these serve not only to increase understanding of life on a given part of the earth's surface. They also help to overcome the excessive compartmentalization in teaching and research that has handicapped the development of Latin American studies and knowledge in general. The barriers to such development are the result of limitations of human time and capacity, in short, to our own underdevelopment. In any case, the many scholars concerned with Latin America are now seeking solid ground between flights of intercontinental journalism and archeological burrowings that are slow to surface.

All of the contributors have had extensive field experience in Latin America and most have been involved in some way in the region's development. James Malloy has recently returned from a year's research and observation in Bolivia. John Gillin has participated periodically in expeditions and field investigations all his life. Dwight Brothers is a member of Harvard's Development Advisory Service. Mr. Powelson has worked with the International Monetary Fund and more recently in the Inter-American Development Bank. Mr. Thorn was a specialist in public finance for the International Monetary Fund and for the OAS. Mr. Cardoso, who began his career in Brazil, has worked in Spanish American countries, such as Chile and Mexico, most recently as an official with the United Nations. José Reyna worked with Cardoso in Chile and is now at the Colegio de México. Mr. Arciniegas has served Colombia as a cabinet member and as an ambassador.

The principal objects of the social change in Latin America with which this volume is concerned are the lower classes. For this reason, John Gillin's essay on the values of these lower classes is not an inappropriate way to lead off the discussion. The opinions and values of the lower classes in Latin America have received only casual and sporadic attention in the past, partly because the views of these groups have had relatively little impact on national life. The views of the middle and upper classes were usually decisive, as they are today. Yet, perhaps one of the most characteristic features of current social change is the increasingly important role played by the new groups.

Ordinarily, the growing concern of the lower classes in improved living standards and a bigger stake in society are discussed as a disturbing element in the body politic. Professor Gillin, however, draws attention to the positive impact of rising expectations on the values of these classes. As new technologies in communication and transportation make greater popular participation in national life possible, the feudal institutions of the countryside are crumbling and peasants are entering the national labor market in increasing numbers. Whereas they formerly had little incentive to work as peons, the peasant immigrants to cities now have fresh incentives, in fact necessities, to work and to acquire consumer goods and other benefits of modern life. Popular demands for better living conditions, according to Professor Gillin, have created a new demand for jobs, and have given increased stature to work as an important lower-class value. The stereotype of the indolent peon snoozing under a tree, sombrero cocked over one eye, is fading into history.

In the next essay Fernando Cardoso and José Luis Reyna give a panoramic survey, supported by some twenty tables of statistics, of the urbanization and industrialization process, and its impact on social structure. The two authors gather together in one place basic data on such matters as the urban and rural mix, growth in per capita output, and occupational groups. The social developments in Latin America that these data describe are compared with similar trends in the United States and Europe during an earlier and comparable period of development.

The Cardoso-Reyna figures document what has already been perceived, namely that the services sector in the more advanced Latin American countries has expanded much more rapidly in the industrializing process and comprises a relatively larger share of the employment, as compared to agriculture and manufacturing, than in the United States or Western Europe. These figures clearly show that for many years the manufacturing sector has continued to occupy roughly the same percentage of the labor force. Much of the emigration from the countryside has, therefore, been absorbed into services, rather than manufacturing. It may come as a surprise that employment in manufacturing, despite sharp absolute increases, has maintained relatively the same level. One is not surprised, however, that the artisan component of manufacturing has dropped sharply while the industrial component has increased correspondingly. Contradicting the widely held view that bureaucratization, that is, a vast expansion of government services, has absorbed immigration to the cities, Cardoso's and Reyna's figures show only a moderate rather than a large increase in the relative numbers of government employees.

Cardoso and Reyna believe that their figures disprove two opposing interpretations. The first is that urbanization and industrialization have resulted in the development of mass societies in Latin America that have a social structure similar to that found in the United States and Western Europe. The fact that the manufacturing sector in Latin America is relatively small tends, in their opinion, to disprove this interpretation. The second interpretation is that Latin America remains essentially a dual society with a traditionally dominant upper class and a large, relatively undifferentiated lower class. On the contrary, Cardoso and Reyna speculate that the dominating sectors of the old agricultural society have made alliances with the new upper strata formed by industrialization. And the old, lower strata are breaking up into different groups, including those which have already joined the industrializing system and those which remain at or outside the periphery. The two authors are disinclined to see two starkly defined groups facing one another. They perceive a not inflexible upper strata adapting, if slowly, to the new conditions and a lower strata developing links with other classes and gradually being absorbed into the economy.

The essays of three economists, John Powelson, Dwight Brothers, and Richard Thorn, form the core of this volume. All three are concerned with conflicts of social philosophy within and between the North and South, public policies on foreign trade and investment, and the impact of both on development.

John Powelson takes his fellow economists, both North and South, to task for different reasons. He believes that the Northern economists' economic views are well founded, but that economic principles alone are insufficient in understanding and implementing economic development. Powelson sympathizes with the political objectives of his Latin American colleagues but suggests that the political variables in their models for economic development be made explicit. He feels that Latin American economists are ill advised to attempt to counter the Northerners' arguments on economic grounds alone. What is at stake are public policies on foreign investment, tariffs, and the role of government in the economy.

In his description of conflicting schools of thought about foreign investment, Dwight Brothers shows how Northern advocacy of free enterprise, free markets, and free international trade and investment are countered in the South by preference for governmental controls and initiatives, suspicion of capitalism and private foreign investment, and a sense of having been victimized by imperialist powers. Brothers feels that we need to know a good deal more about how the gains from foreign investment are distributed, that is, whether local interests are, in fact, being victimized. He also points out that research is needed on the impact of foreign investment on trade, payments, and economic development. In the meantime, he advocates caution about artificial government stimuli for encouraging reluctant investors in this country to invest abroad or to force Latin Americans to accept investments about which they are leery. Brothers maintains that Latin American countries themselves must decide what foreign investment they receive and on what terms, just as the private investors should judge investment opportunities on their own merits. He maintains this view in the face of unilateral efforts to stimulate such investment, particularly since capital flows to the private sectors have fallen far short of the goals originally established under the Alliance for Progress.

Richard Thorn views the Alliance as more significant for the economic and social goals established, than in the actual progress achieved towards these goals. As for the overall rate of growth of per capita income, Latin America as a whole did poorly during 1961–1965: only 1.4 percent per annum. The performance of Argentina and Brazil brought the average down, and seven countries exceeded the growth target of 2.5 percent. The record of achievement was mixed in the social field as well. Thorn conceives of the problem of the Alliance not so much in terms of material achievements as in terms of progress towards consensus and experience gained in multinational planning and organization. In short, Thorn suggests that the major problem of the Alliance is political insofar as the crucial element is a clear understanding of goals, and greater common determination and more effective organization to achieve them.

In the last two essays Germán Arciniegas and James Malloy are concerned with politics; the former discusses its interaction with culture, and the latter its relation to economic development.

Mr. Arciniegas explains that poets, philosophers, and artists have traditionally been active in politics because resistance to Spanish domination in the colonial period grew up in the universities and because later opposition to dictators could sometimes find expression only in literature and the arts. Among the political leaders distinguished in the humanities whom Arciniegas singles out are José Martí, Rómulo Gallegos, and Jaime Torres Bodet. The sparkling facets of Arciniegas' essay catch reflections of the prosaic concerns of earlier chapters.

In his study of the Bolivian revolution, James Malloy singles out economic development as a major objective of the revolutionary leadership. Yet, in order to maintain needed popular support, the revolutionary government was forced to distribute rather than save resources needed for investment. According to Malloy, the Bolivian revolutionaries never succeeded in securing a strong enough political position to implement their plans for economic development. On the one hand, support groups such as labor and the peasants succeeded in preventing the government from taking the harsh measures necessary for rapid accumulation of capital. As a result, in its twelve years in office the revolutionary movement did not succeed in achieving economic growth sufficient to provide the surpluses that these groups demanded. Unlike the Soviet and Chinese revolutionary leadership, the Bolivians were either unable or unwilling to use the totalitarian methods that have driven many Communist states up the rocky slope of industrialization. While Malloy does not reach the dismal conclusion that rapid economic development can only be reached in a totalitarian setting, he does conclude that once the Bolivian revolutionary leadership lost the ability to use force on behalf of its ideological model, the unreconciled conflict between demands for consumption as against investment led to political and economic decline.

The title of this volume contains a loaded word, "constructive," about whose meaning there is insufficient common agreement. Yet, one of the purposes of this volume is to permit scholars from a variety of disciplines to point the way they believe Americans from North and South should go. All of the authors do, of course, attribute importance to improved living standards and increased output. What is less commonplace is the emphasis they all place on the need to foster social consensus. In fact, the core of the constructive change that is most needed may be progress towards such consensus.

Professor Gillin is concerned with values as they relate to consensus, particularly on the part of the lower classes whose views have traditionally been politically irrelevant. Cardoso and Reyna deal with the occupational and sectoral fissures that underlie conflicting interests and goals. Mr. Powelson is less concerned with Latin American consensus on economic matters—which is fairly strong, particularly in regard to industrialized countries—than in establishing a better understanding between Latin America and the United States. Similarly, Dwight Brothers seeks to define a proper and constructive role for private capital in Latin America, an area where controversy and apparently conflicting influences tend to paralyze constructive effort. Richard Thorn sees the absence of real consensus, as opposed to apparent consensus, as a major problem of the Alliance especially since such consensus and the determination to implement goals effectively is indispensable to its success. Germán Arciniegas' essay highlights the philosophical and political contradictions within Latin American society, often so intense that only poets and novelists are capable of coping with them. James Malloy shows how competing interests within a revolutionary society, torn and bleeding in its break from the past, prevented the establishment of national policies involving the hard choices required for rapid economic development.

As these essays show, progress towards consensus in Latin America has been painful and slow. Nonetheless, the march of events in most countries focuses public attention more and more on the common man's needs and aspirations. His interests are being taken into account now more than ever before.

Cole Blasier, Director
Center for Latin American Studies
University of Pittsburgh

CONSTRUCTIVE

CHANGE IN

LATIN AMERICA

JOHN P. GILLIN

Changing Cultural Values of the Latin American Lower Classes

T H E rising tide of wants and expectations is being felt by many of the lower classes in Latin America. To continue the figure, they are becoming increasingly anxious about keeping their noses above water while rising with the tide. It is essential that United States policy-makers understand these matters and prepare programs that offer the working classes some tangible basis for hope, for Communists and their co-workers are everywhere trying to take advantage of the newly developing dissatisfactions among the lower strata. Violent revolution is, of course, one of the instruments they advocate for transforming the region into a "workers' paradise."

My "home town" in Guatemala, where I have done much field work, illustrates the changing values among Latin American lower

John P. Gillin is Research Professor of Anthropology in the University of Pittsburgh.

1

classes. This is a community, far from the tourist areas of the country, whose members are about two-third Pokomam Indians and one-third Ladinos (nationals, usually *mestizos*). The Indians are considered a lower caste and most of the Ladinos are rated by the sixteen "society" families as lower class. I have spent many seasons there, but eight years had intervened between the last visit and one made in 1964. Because it was Holy Week, most people were dressed up and showing off their best. I saw some things among the lower-class Ladinos and Indians that I had never associated with them, changes that indicated new wants and values.

Many of the men were wearing permanently creased trousers with cuffs, modern style shirts with collars and neckties, and wristwatches. Some of the young women were in modern knee-length dresses with silk stockings and high-heeled shoes, and several had rather strange-looking coiffures indicating attempts at permanent waves. Practically all of these people were illiterate and did not read newspapers, magazines, or have access to other forms of visible advertising. They did not have television sets. How did they find out about these new things? Many of the people had acquired small transistor radios, made in Japan, selling for about five dollars. They carried them in their hands or pockets, and the little receivers spewed forth musical entertainment, interrupted about every ten minutes by descriptions of the good things people could easily get if they would just scrape together a few cents or dollars. Even in a backwoods country town like this one, which did not have a department store, traveling traders brought many of these factory-produced goods to the weekly public markets.

Electronic communications and other media had stimulated other wants as well. The church, which in former days enjoyed a visit from a priest only once every month or six weeks, now had a full-time, educated clergyman who focused mainly on the common people rather than the "society" families. On top of the great stone church building, erected in 1680, there was now an electric loudspeaker, which advocated, in a fairly "popular" fashion, hard work, better education, and religious devotion. The community, with help from the Agency for International Development, had built a new six-year school, which offered special classes for Indian youngsters to perfect their Spanish so that they could continue school rather than dropping out, as formerly. The new generation of young men and women should be fairly literate and effectively exposed to printed ideas and advertising. A Peace Corps contingent of three young North Americans was showing people that it was fairly easy to dig wells and have fresh, pure water in place of water from public fountains supplied by the local creek.

There is no need to go into more details. The peasants and hand laborers of this community had developed some new wants and values they had never heard of before or had previously considered out of reach. This particular community is not typical of lower-class culture throughout Latin America, but the observations of other investigators and travelers indicate that similar or parallel changes are taking place in both rural and urban situations in most parts of Latin America.

Elsewhere[1] I have discussed some of the main cultural values of the Latin American middle sectors. Here I should like to suggest certain values that seem to be important among the lower classes of the modern Latin American societies. Since there is considerable variation throughout the different countries and a paucity of thorough studies of the lower-status categories, these remarks will be in part suggestive rather than definitive. I hope that they will stimulate further investigation.[2] Recognized native Indian groups that have not fully entered the national society and that still maintain their own cultures or subcultures are not considered in what follows.

A few general remarks are in order before going into some of these values. First, although the general culture of Latin America has its roots in Western civilization, it should be distinguished from the Anglo-American culture represented by Canada and the United

States. Second, the Latin American countries are emerging nations. They have emerged a good deal farther into the modern world than most of the ex-colonies of Africa and Asia, but they are not as fully developed as Western Europe, Anglo-America, New Zealand, and Australia. Third, it is, I believe, a mistake for members of the developed nations to expect the Latin American countries (or the area as a whole) to make themselves into carbon copies of any one of the developed sociocultural systems. Differences in historical background and in natural environments militate against this and indicate that Latin America will still have some peculiarities of its own when more fully developed. This is particularly important if North Americans are to develop with their southern neighbors a full partnership in the western hemisphere. There is a tendency among some "Yankees" to think that if we give aid to the Latin Americans they should turn themselves into Spanish- or Portuguese-speaking versions of ourselves.

Many parts of Latin America are changing quite rapidly in various ways. But the most ubiquitous change for the area as a whole is in size of population. Most experts agree that it has the fastest growing population of any of the major areas of the world, averaging at least 3.0 percent growth per year. The greatest bulge is in those sections of the population known as the lower classes.

The Latin American lower classes fall into several types. Those who live in *rural* areas may be (1) small farmers who cultivate their own land either full- or part-time; (2) peons attached to large haciendas either by debt or some other arrangement that obligates them to work at least part-time for the owner or manager of the large estate; (3) wage-paid workers in large industrialized agricultural enterprises, so-called factories in the fields such as sugar refineries, fruit-growing and fruit-processing estates, large coffee-growing and coffee-preparation businesses, etc.; (4) workers in extractive industries such as mines and oil fields; and (5) free-floating rural labor not permanently attached to any given place. In some areas part of the rural lower class live in separate residences in the open countryside,[3] although usually within walking or donkey-riding distance of a village with a market, church, and local government office. More commonly they live in settlements and go out to work on the land during the day. The "factories in the fields" usually provide barracks-like buildings, where families as well as single workers live, plus a company store or trading post and perhaps a chapel. Some American concerns, such as the United Fruit Company and various mining companies, provide settlements with dwellings, sports fields, and schools, and with piped water, sewage, and other public utilities. These settlements have been imitated here and there by local enterprises.

Lower-class people who live in cities (as distinguished from small towns) are of two general types: (1) "old-time" urban workers, who usually live in permanently built, although often very crowded, dwellings in restricted parts of the city (where middle- and upper-class families do not live), and (2) recent immigrants from the rural areas, who crowd into makeshift shantytowns, usually on the outskirts of the cities. The latter segment of the urban lower classes poses the greatest problems at present. The slum dwellers crowd into the cities looking for work because of the population explosion in the rural regions and in some areas because the owners or proprietors of rural land restrict its use.

Now let us consider briefly some of the cultural values held by the lower classes. I shall venture to indicate what to me seem to be some indications of change. Only time will tell whether my assumptions are correct.

Work

The lower classes, generally speaking, are not lazy, but place high value upon labor with hands and muscles, when they can get it and when they receive adequate compensation for it. The middle and upper strata disdain this type of work. Such an attitude presents a contrast to North America, where middle-class men are not ashamed to be seen pushing a lawn mower, fixing a broken step on the porch, or doing many other chores requiring hands and muscles, at least about their homes.

In Latin America all unskilled manual laborers, male and female, are of lower-class status. Also included in this status are many persons North Americans would call skilled workers, although in Latin America such workers may be illiterate. Thus, for example, chauffeurs, tractor operators, masons, carpenters, mechanics, seamstresses, and other artisans who work with their hands are usually rated in the lower classes. Various reports indicate that students tend to shun higher education in fields such as mechanical engineering, which require one to work with wrenches and nuts and bolts, for fear that such work would degrade their social standing. To be sure, some of the lower class work their way up into at least the lower levels of the middle segments by becoming literate and acquiring skills that enable them to give up manual labor.

However, work is sought by the lower classes to provide subsistence for themselves and dependents and to pay for some of the "rising tide of expectations." Most Latin American governments, even dictatorships, at one time or another have at least gone through the motions of providing jobs in public works, setting up minimum wage rates in certain fields, and providing medical and hospital assistance for workers. Labor unions in Latin America have been organized almost everywhere among certain types of workers, although their programs have usually been more politically oriented than in the United States and Canada. An international organization of non-Communist unions, Organización Regional Internacional de Trabajadores (O.R.I.T), cooperates with the North American A.F.L.–C.I.O. Leftist or Marxist unions have an international affiliation in the Confederación de Trabajadores de la América Latina

(C.T.A.L) under the leadership of the Mexican, Lombardo Toledano.

Today, the high value placed on jobs among the lower classes results from several factors: (1) The great majority of people in all Latin American countries subsist on income derived from their own labor; (2) the continuing population explosion demands an increasing number of jobs; (3) in many areas land is held out of cultivation for speculative purposes or for grazing, or because, even uncultivated, it provides the owners of large estates with sufficient income for luxurious living, regardless of the fate of the workers; (4) industry has not developed sufficiently to absorb the growing numbers of lower-class workers.

Women

In the Latin American lower classes, women have a higher value than women in the middle and upper classes, although this is not always explicitly admitted by informants. For one thing, women's earning ability, although it may be small, is essential for the maintenance of most lower-class families. The wife and mother is the anchor of most of these families. Consensual "marriage," unrecognized by law or church, is much more common than in the higher classes, and there is a greater tendency for the husband to desert the family, leaving to the wife and mother the responsibility for the support and care of the children. She may receive the help of relatives and friends until she finds another man, but the responsibility is hers. A somewhat similar situation is said to exist in certain Negro rural and city slums in the United States. Even in permanent marriages the lower-class Latin American wife has more independence than women of higher status because she is usually out of the home more, without chaperonage or other familial supervision.

Land

Because the larger part of the lower class is, or recently has been, dependent upon what it can earn by agricultural labor, land has a high value. Redistribution of land and reform of the system of ownership and exploitation are among the important objectives of all programs appealing to the lower strata. Most economists see land reform as essential for increasing the area's productivity and independence in world markets. Mexico, under the constitution of 1917, was the first Latin American nation to divide most of its large privately held haciendas among the workers, either individually or in cooperatives called *ejidos*. Bolivia, in the revolution of the early 1950's, also instituted large-scale land reform (as well as nationalization of its largest mines). As a result of the recognition of economies and other factors and the dissemination of information on the subject, land reform has acquired to some degree a high value among the workers and among liberal-minded planners in practically all areas.

The worker's desire to work his own land or to have a stake in what he works must be balanced against national and regional economic problems. For example, in most areas if an agricultural worker is given a small patch of his own, say ten acres, he will produce no more than subsistence for himself and family. He will not be able to use higher income-producing farming methods, machinery, or manufactured fertilizer, and will sell his surplus products, if any, on a small scale, and for less profit than he would in large-scale market operations. For these reasons, fairly large cooperative farms, in which each peasant owns a nonsalable stake, are thought by many experts to be most effective.

On the other hand, expropriation of large feudalistic estates without paying the owners can also cause unrest and violence and, in the long run, be politically and economically detrimental to a country. One solution, where it is possible, is for the government to pay the owner a reasonable price, stipulating that the money be invested in an industrial enterprise within the country. In this way, capital can be kept from flowing out of the country and economic balance will eventually be achieved. Not only can large private, monopolistic estates be converted into cooperatives of workers, but in some areas much unoccupied, nationally owned land can also be so developed. An example is land on the lower western slopes of the Andes in Ecuador, which is being internally colonized in this manner. In parts of Central America the North American fruit companies are turning some of their lowland tropical estates over to cooperatives, which will grow the bananas and other products that the companies will in turn buy and transport to foreign markets.

Personalism

The lower classes share certain cultural values with the middle and upper strata, although these values differ in details and in focus. Personalism is one of them, and it is still important. The lower-class person believes that he and others have a unique inner dignity (*dignidad de la persona*), which must be respected by others, including people of the higher levels of society. *Machismo* (maleness) is one aspect of personalism. A real man, by Latin American standards, should be prepared to defend his dignity by force if necessary. He should also assert his sexual virility by having a girl friend other than his wife, or more than one wife. Although *machismo* is applicable to the lower classes, it is perhaps more characteristic of other classes. Oscar Lewis writes that "*machismo* is much weaker in rural areas than in the cities and weaker among the lower classes than in the middle and upper classes."[4]

Personalism also involves developing close friendships among individuals and among families of the same class. Daily borrowing, lending, and other forms of mutual aid are common within circles of friends. Also lower-class people try to have *patrones* or friends in the higher levels of society. A *patrón* does not mingle with his lower-class friends on an equal basis, but he is supposed to do them favors in return for work, political support, and other forms of reciprocity.

Personalism is also a necessary aspect of social intercourse in many aspects of life for the lower classes—for example, in religion, economic life, and politics. If most lower-class Latin Americans are "good Catholics," it is not because of their attachment to the ideological or theological aspects of Christianity. If they are active in the church, it is usually because of personal attachment to a priest or other religious worker. A lower-class person may also have a close attachment to a saint. In large business and agricultural enterprises it is often impossible for the owner or top executive to develop his relationship as *patrón* with all his workers, but the latter seek *patrones* among the lower-grade boss-men or among union labor leaders. Political leaders try to develop and maintain this type of friendship among their lower-class constituents, who often do not care about or do not understand the enunciated political programs. It is usually difficult to secure wholehearted cooperation from members of the lower class on an impersonal basis.

As education spreads and the common people have an opportunity to learn of the nonpersonalistic or general social values involved in various sociocultural institutions, this sort of personalistic approach will probably decline. But at present, for most such people, the theoretical appeals of both Communism and democracy, as understood in the universities, have little appeal; it is the practical side of political theories and systems that create appeal, as do the personalities of their protagonists.

Festivity

All Latin Americans enjoy parties or fiestas and, generally speaking, engage in them more frequently than the average North American. Birthdays and other saints' days are celebrated frequently throughout the year, as well as holidays commemorating political and military events. In the case of community-wide or national celebrations lower-class people usually participate in parades and other public affairs. They are not, of course, included in the private parties of the other classes, but they usually organize their own family or community parties. Many lower-class people play musical instruments, which together with general singing and dancing form part of the entertainment. A great deal of alcohol is usually consumed.

North American observers have pointed out that the lower classes would have more money to buy "essentials" if they did not spend so much on periodic merrymaking. But the lower-class Latin American considers frequent fiestas necessary to offset the drabness of his daily life. To him freedom from boredom is one of the essentials of life.

As education and per capita income increase, the forms of festivity will likely change. One innovation in some areas is the inclusion of team sports such as soccer, football, and basketball.

Living Standards

Should material conditions improve, some of the present lower classes will lose a certain picturesqueness. Many romanticists hate to see factory-made cloth replacing that woven in the home, ready-made clothes instead of those sewn by the women, store-bought dishes rather than homemade pottery, shoes instead of sandals, factory-made stoves instead of charcoal burners, radio and phonograph music crowding out the amateur musicians, and so on. Nonetheless, if incomes are increased, there is little doubt that the Latin American lower classes will be "in the market" for at least some changes in their way of life. In the opinion of most experts, however, the chances of most of the Latin American lower classes being able to make these changes are slight unless two changes take place. First, the population explosion must be brought under control.

Second, wealth as a whole must increase and be better distributed. Industrialization and a more equitable distribution of productive land seem to be the general answers here, and let us hope that they will not require violent revolutions for their accomplishment.

Four of the values from this tentative list are long established and go back to colonial times. These are the values placed on the woman as anchor of the household, on land, on personalism, and on festivity. On the other hand, work had little value in itself as long as it consisted merely of peonage; nor were improved living standards a cultural value among the lower classes as long as they seemed frozen to a condition of mere subsistence and there were no opportunities for gaining what the middle and upper classes already possessed. Social democratic political programs, the drive of modern business to increase the consumer goods market, and improved communications among the lower classes and between them and the rest of society have helped to raise the value placed on work and improved living standards. These and other sociocultural changes may well lead to new values in the days to come.

One peculiarity of lower-class Latin Americans as compared with North Americans of similar status has been a lack of political patriotism, i.e., being aware of one's country and sharing, at least in part, its value system. Numerous other observers, as well as myself, have been in isolated sections of Latin America where the common people did not have the faintest idea of the country to which they belonged, who its neighbors were, and so on. The provincial political officials were aware of such things, but often in only a rudimentary way. Again, I think we can predict a change in this respect as literacy and access to electronic communications proceed among the lower classes. Attachment to principles, rather than to *patrones* or bossmen, will, it is hoped, come to characterize both the politicians and the lower-class voters. Likewise police and other forms of force will be used more to maintain law and order than for political purposes.

One of the negative values of most lower-class Latin Americans has to do with their atitude toward the military. (Costa Rica is the only country which does not have an army.) The national police have often been a source of repression and threat (for example, in elections). And the army, into which many lower-class men are drafted, offers neither social nor economic benefits, for such men, being illiterate, have little chance of becoming even noncommissioned officers. In recent years there have been a few border wars such as the Chaco war between Paraguay and Bolivia, and there has been bloodshed over the Ecuadorean-Peruvian boundary lines. But for the most part, the Latin American armies are insignificant forces in world affairs. Brazil sent a few troops to fight on the Allied side in Italy during World War II, and Colombia sent some soldiers to fight on the American side in Korea. Only three countries sent token forces to join the United States forces in "keeping the peace" in the Dominican Republic in 1965.

In short, the Latin American military in many countries is an internal political force rather than an instrument of national policy determined by the voters and civilian officials. In mid-1966, a military junta ousted the elected civilian president in Argentina, and in Guatemala the military, which had overthrown an elected president, has just released the top executive office to an elected civilian. There is much cynical discussion as to how long he will last. Military dictators have been part of the history of all Latin American countries. They are usually conservative and little concerned, except for occasional symbolic displays, with the welfare of the lower classes. It is little wonder that the lower classes, with their growing awareness of nationhood and the possibilities of achieving a higher standard of living, either respond to the government with a certain numbness or join guerilla bands.

Most of the lower-class people crowding into the urban shantytowns want jobs. Although growing public and private services provide some employment, what is badly needed in most Latin

American countries are more manufacturing industries, not only to provide work, but also to balance the economies. For the time being, the type of industry desirable is that concerned with making consumer goods. Most heavy basic industries, such as steel plants, are uneconomical in many countries as presently constituted. Such heavy industry should be organized on a regional basis involving the cooperation of several nations, as in the Central American Common Market. But most countries, even small ones like Costa Rica and Ecuador, could support more consumer goods industries, which would not only provide jobs but would also conserve foreign exchange. Millions of dollars flow out each year to pay for foreign manufactured items such as pots and pans, modern stoves, cloth, garments, radio receivers, bicycles, small motors, small agricultural equipment, and so on and on.

Even small industries require capital to get started, and most of the foreigners who import small manufactured goods are not anxious to supply it. In the absence of capital from foreign investors, two possibilities exist. One, already mentioned, is government breakup of large haciendas and the requirement that money paid for them be invested in industry. Second, agencies such as the Alliance for Progress could provide more long-term loans for establishing industries. Some United States businesses will not care for this procedure since it provides competition for their products (often sold at exorbitant prices) in Latin America. But in the long run, U.S. business would benefit, I believe, because the local availability of certain items would undoubtedly increase wants for other things which the United States could supply profitably.

If Latin American countries can expand and increase manufactured products, a new value would develop among the lower classes. We can call this *economic patriotism*. At one time, we had the same kind of patriotism in our country. When I was a young boy, I earned spending-money by planting and caring for the flower gardens of two elderly women in the neighborhood. I remember being told,

"Don't buy those hoes and rakes made in England. They're no good. Take those that were made in this country, right in Chicago." This may have been true or false, but it built up in me, as in other young people, a patriotism that favored buying United States goods. Latin American countries could use a bit more of this.

However, it is difficult to see how the Latin American lower classes can come near to satisfying their growing wants, unless some fundamental changes are made in the sociocultural systems. At present the average family in this class receives annually about $250 in cash income. In some countries and regions it is somewhat more, in others less. (This figure does not include food and housing of most rural workers.) In the United States in 1966 an income of less than $3,000 placed a family in the poverty class. Obviously the lower classes of Latin America cannot purchase with their incomes any appreciable amount of the good things of life they see or hear advertised, regardless of the differences in family financing as compared with the United States.

As Frank Tannenbaum has written:

The United States was indifferent to the social and political consequences of the consumer's revolution we have spread across the face of the earth. Ours is a peculiarly ingratiating revolution—painless, pleasant, and irresistible. . . . Americans are unaware of their role as the gravedigger of class-ridden and stratified societies. They are selling toothpaste, fountain pens, and modern plumbing. In fact, however, they are undermining the stratified society characteristic of Latin America and much of the rest of the world.[5]

In effect, as Tannenbaum and others have pointed out, we are promoting a nonpolitical but far-reaching social revolution simply by producing and trying to sell what we ourselves, and other people all over the world, Latin America included, regard as the "good things of life." Whether this revolution can continue without troublesome social and political consequences is one of the most important problems the United States must face.

It is well known that the promoters of another type of revolution, the Communists, are ready and willing to step into any void or area of discontent that may develop. According to reliable reports, the one country in Latin America where Communism has taken over, Cuba, has not enjoyed a rising standard of living or access on the part of the common people to material goods. Quite the opposite. The economy has had to be sustained by enormous loans from Russia, and, to some extent, by the impressment of forced labor to produce sugar. Rather than developing local manufactures and a higher production of consumer goods, Cuba has become more than ever a one-crop economy with shortages of everything from automobile parts to workers' footwear.

The "free enterprise revolution" of the United States has not been planned or executed with design. In spite of the benefits to developing countries it has carried with it, it has many defects that critics have been only too ready to point out. For example, many companies operating in Latin America have now and then established monopolistic controls in certain areas; they have occasionally indulged in under-the-table deals with local officials regarding wages, taxes, and tariffs; and they have often been guided more by prospects of their own profits than by the requirements of general economic and social development of the countries in which they were operating. The North American free enterprise revolution, however, has not been monolithic, centrally planned, and controlled in the same way as exported Communism—or exported Nazism in the days of Adolf Hitler. With understanding and planning the United States could help promote and support a peaceful sociocultural revolution in Latin America, one that would bring our neighbors to what we regard as a decent standard of living. The Alliance for Progress is a step in this direction, but it seems to have yet produced neither important land reforms nor significant growth of local industry.

I realize that "revolution" has an uncomfortable connotation in the United States, but it is becoming increasingly necessary that competent authorities and experts on our side give serious attention to planning and carrying out a social revolution in Latin America that will constructively bring the poor into the national picture of their countries and provide them with the material goods which many of them are now aware of and for which they yearn.

Notes and References

1. "Some Signposts for Policy," in Richard N. Adams *et al., Social Change in Latin America Today: Its Implications for United States Policy*, New York: Harpers [for the Council on Foreign Relations], 1960, pp. 14–62 (Vintage edition, New York: 1961); also, "Cultura emergente," in J. L. Arriola, ed., *Integración social en Guatemala*, Guatemala: Editorial del Ministro de Educación Publica, 1956, pp. 435–57; "Components of the Ethos in Modern Latin American Culture," *American Anthropologist*, Vol. 57 (1955), pp. 488–500.

2. The outstanding student of the Latin American urban lower class has been Oscar Lewis. His investigations of such people have been made largely in Mexico City and Puerto Rico.

3. Moche, Peru is an example. See John Gillin, *Moche: A Peruvian Coastal Community*, Washington, D. C.: Institute of Social Anthropology, Smithsonian Institution (Publ. 3), 1947.

4. Oscar Lewis, *Five Families*, New York: Basic Books, 1959, p. 17.

5. Frank Tannenbaum, *Ten Keys to Latin America*, New York: Knopf, 1962, pp. 201, 203.

FERNANDO H. CARDOSO

JOSE LUIS REYNA

Industrialization, Occupational Structure, and Social Stratification in Latin America

S PECIALIZED sociological literature analyzing Latin American development has focused on the so-called obstacles to change or on social forces capable of alleviating stagnation and underdevelopment. Some of the principal hypotheses concerned with the social conditions of development and many of the essays written on the Latin American social situation assume the existence of a traditionally dominant, oligarchical, and, according to some authors, aristocratic class controlling the political and economic system of the region. To such writers the traditional class appears to be opposing change. At the same time the idea has evolved that the "mobilized but unincorporated" masses constitute the dynamic basis of the political and social

Fernando H. Cardoso is former Deputy Director of the Social Development Planning Division in the Latin American Institute for Economic and Social Planning. José Luis Reyna is Research Associate at El Colegio de México.

system. These masses are conceived, according to the ideological preferences of the analysts, as a "potential class" or "citizens masses" governed by the motives and orientations of consumption (which the "demonstration effect" of developed countries stimulates) or as "marginal masses" threatening the existing society, just as in the past the "barbarians" threatened Western civilization.

There has also been much emphasis on the supposed effects of the development process on the Latin American social situation, namely, that insufficient dynamism of economic development becomes apparent in the inability of the productive system to create enough employment to absorb the demographic growth of the region. Consequently, whenever industrialization begins or when urbanization is accelerated, the typical conditions of underdevelopment become immediately apparent. These conditions are there in the society and economy, but as long as the patterns of agrarian economy prevail they are not dramatically revealed. Industrialization and urbanization make the precariousness of the prevailing situation apparent. Thus, vast expanses of *favelas, barriadas, callampas*, or whatever other name is given to miserable living areas, makes vividly apparent the low standard of living—involving health, housing, and education—of a substantial portion of the population in the cities. If to these considerations is added the high rate of population growth of rural areas and of the lower urban strata, it is easy to understand why frequently the dynamic potential of popular discontentment is said to add to the rigidity ascribed to the traditional political and social establishment.

However, and without denying the situation of want in which the larger part of the population actually lives (there is even a tendency for the absolute numbers of people living under substandard conditions to increase), a careful evaluation of the magnitude, range, and significance of the changes that have occurred in Latin America during recent decades seems to be appropriate. Obviously, such changes will vary significantly from country to country and will show up in different social and economic levels, both in the demographic and occupational structures and in the productive system.

In this paper an attempt will be made to identify these transformations on the basis of the information available. In order to avoid the mistake of talking generically of Latin America, as if it were a region affected by homogeneous problems and sharing similar perspectives, attention will be focused on only a few countries. As selective criteria, a basic dimension was chosen: the degree of development of the industrial-productive system. Therefore, the specific purpose of this paper will be to determine the transformations that occurred in the socioeconomic structure of those Latin American countries most industrialized, selected according to the availability of pertinent statistics.

Analysis of such data shows that the traditional image of the region as one politically controlled by classes little inclined to modernize does not readily correspond to the actual situation in the countries under consideration. Furthermore, the data demonstrate that one should not assume that during the development process the same patterns are being repeated that once characterized the evolution of today's older industrialized countries. In the latter, industrialization operated autonomously; in the countries being studied it follows a pattern in which the technical-economic advancement of the older industrialized countries imposes certain norms. Although there have been structural changes, some rather accelerated and with deep effects, the data do not uphold the hypothesis that industrial advancement and socioeconomic transformation—even in the more developed countries in the region—have achieved social and economic integration patterns similar to those prevailing in developed countries. The available data suggest hypotheses about changes in social and political integration patterns that are perhaps more realistic.

Throughout this paper an attempt will be made to pinpoint

some features of the emerging social structure which diminish the validity of the hypotheses upholding the "oligarchy-people" pattern—and of hypotheses assuming modernization of the region in terms of the formation of "mass industrial societies." The final section will present a possible interpretation of the type of development now being achieved in Latin America. In the long run, the perspective of this paper emphasizes that the social and economic changes in Latin America are considerable.

STRUCTURAL CHANGES IN LATIN AMERICA

The change experienced by Latin America during recent years, although it has differing connotations in each country, has manifested some general tendencies in the area as a whole. These manifestations can be appraised in various dimensions. For the purposes of this study the most significant are urbanization, composition of the employed population, and the evolution of industrial production.

The Urbanization Process

Between 1925 and 1962 Latin America was characterized by rapid urban growth, mainly due to migration from rural to urban areas. Table 1 illustrates this phenomenon. Even though the rural population increased numerically during this period, in percentage terms the urban population increased substantially with respect to the rural.

In 1925 over two-thirds of the population lived in towns of less than 2,000 inhabitants, whereas in 1962 almost half of the population lived in urban centers of over 2,000 inhabitants. Besides, the population increase rate is higher in capitals and larger cities (100,000 inhabitants and over); in the long run, this causes noticeable modifications in the behavior of social groups.

Between 1925 and 1950 rural population decreased more or less noticeably, a trend which became intensified in the 1950–60 decade.[1] During the "import substitution" period this process accelerated. Nevertheless, the rhythm of urban growth surpasses that of industrial development in Latin America, and in some cases there is urbanization without industrialization.

TABLE 1

CHANGES IN URBAN AND RURAL POPULATION, LATIN AMERICA, 1925–62
(Percentages)

	1925	1950	1955	1960	1962
Rural	70.5	60.7	57.3	53.9	52.6
Urban[a]	29.5	39.3	42.7	46.1	47.4
	100.0%	100.0%	100.0%	100.0%	100.0%
	(92,869)[b]	(156,146)	(178,880)	(205,941)	(217,826)

a. "Urban" refers to localities of more than 2,000 inhabitants.
b. In thousands of persons; percentages were extracted from the totals.
SOURCE: Z. Slawinski, "Los cambios estructurales del empleo en el desarrollo de América Latina," *Boletín económico de América Latina*, X, No. 2 (October 1965), p. 161.

Employed Population

Paralleling the urbanization process during this period, changes occurred in the structure of the employed population. The obvious result of a diminishing rural population and an increasing urban one is a decrease of the active population engaged in farming and an increase in the nonfarming sectors (Table 2). The new population sectors being formed, due in part to the rural-urban migratory movement, were absorbed chiefly by the services sector (tertiary), which indicates that in Latin America growth of the industrial sector (secondary) follows a relatively slower rhythm than that of the tertiary.

Indeed, Table 3 shows that the manufacturing sector, although it was growing during the thirty-five years under scrutiny, remained practically static in terms of percentages. However, in spite of this relative stability, the artisan sector shrank and the industrial developed. The increase of the construction sector is also considerable. The nonmanufacturing sectors grew even faster, as can be seen by looking at the respective figures for the "basic services," "business and finance," and "miscellaneous services" sectors. It is

TABLE 2

Changes in Employment, Latin America, 1925–62

(Percentages)

	1925	1950	1955	1960	1962
Farming	61.3	53.1	50.0	47.3	46.1
Nonfarming	38.7	46.9	50.0	52.7	53.9
	100.0%	100.0%	100.0%	100.0%	100.0%
	(19,913)[a]	(28,235)	(30,301)	(32,360)	(33,190)

a. In thousands of persons; percentages were extracted from the totals.
SOURCE: Slawinski, p. 161.

TABLE 3

Distribution of Nonagricultural Employment, Latin America, 1925–60

(Percentages)

	1925	1950	1960
Mining	1.0	1.1	1.0
Manufacturing	13.7	14.4	14.3
Industrial	(3.5)	(6.9)	(7.5)
Artisan	(10.2)	(7.5)	(6.8)
Construction	1.6	3.7	4.9
Basic services	3.2	4.2	5.2
Trade and finance	6.7	7.9	9.2
Government	2.2	3.3	3.7
Miscellaneous services	7.9	9.9	12.1
Unspecified activities	2.4	2.4	2.3
	38.7%	46.9%	52.7%

SOURCE: Slawinski, p. 164.

noticeable that not all of the population migrating from the rural to the urban sector, where the main source of new occupation development is considered to be, was absorbed, but remained marginal to the economic system.

Because of the diminishing importance of the rural sector and the resulting predominance of the urban sector, it can be inferred that the traditional system of domination based on the hacienda has somewhat lost its significance, or is taking a new form.

Evolution of Industrial Production

The productive structure of the region also experienced appreciable transformation. For the purpose of this paper, the most significant modification was the increasing importance of the industrial sector within the economy as a whole. Although the growth of this sector was less than that of the nonmanufacturing sector, the changes are undeniable. Obviously, the manner of the expansion of the industrial sector has not been the same for the various countries. There are some apparent differences, which makes it possible to establish three large categories of countries:

1. Countries of relatively long-established industrialization
2. Countries of recent industrialization
3. Countries of an incipient degree of industrialization

Table 4 reflects the different stages of growth over thirty years, based on these categories. The first group of countries—those of "old" industrialization—continued the process with a per capita growth rate of approximately 100 percent between 1930 and 1960 (almost doubling in Argentina and Uruguay and more than doubling in Chile). The second group—countries of more recent industrialization—experienced an even more pronounced growth of approximately three to four times the initial rate. This was not so in the third group, which started out with very low production and did not achieve any considerable overall growth during the 1930–60 period.

Because of these trends, the following discussion will consider the countries listed in the first two groups of Table 4, in which it is possible to speak of an industrial economy. The last country of

TABLE 4

EVOLUTION OF PER CAPITA INDUSTRIAL PRODUCTION
IN 18 LATIN AMERICAN COUNTRIES, 1930–60

(Per capita product generated in the manufacturing
sector in 1960 U.S. dollars)

Group I	1930	1940	1950	1960
Argentina	152.5	172.6	234.0	277.0
Chile	44.2	54.3	98.2	108.5
Uruguay	97.9a	84.7	130.6	164.0
Group II				
Brazil	24.8	32.9	56.8	101.6
Colombia	13.0	23.6	42.8	60.5
Mexico	34.4	46.2	65.2	112.1
Peru	b	b	36.2	56.1
Venezuela	b	38.0	51.3	87.6
Costa Rica	b	b	45.4	57.5
Group III				
Bolivia	b	b	26.6	20.1
Ecuador	b	23.7	34.4	40.5
El Salvador	b	b	15.7	16.4
Guatemala	b	b	22.0	24.1
Haiti	b	b	8.8	9.5
Honduras	9.9	10.4	15.8	22.6
Nicaragua	b	b	21.7	30.9
Panama	b	b	33.6	43.0
Paraguay	b	b	53.3	47.1

a. For 1935.

b. Data not available.

SOURCE: Simposio Latinoamericano de Industrialización, *El proceso de industrialización en América Latina,* Anexo estadístico, Santiago: Comisión Económica para América Latina (CEPAL), 1966, p. 23.

NOTE: Cuba and the Dominican Republic are excluded for lack of data.

each of the two groups (Uruguay and Costa Rica) will not be discussed since their economies represent considerable deviations from the historical evolution within their respective groups.

An initial analysis of change and industrialization will be made on the basis of two dimensions: (1) per capita net product, defined as the ratio between the gross domestic product and the number of inhabitants, and (2) urbanization, which will consider populations in places of over 2,000 inhabitants. Special attention will be given to the changes occurring in the occupational structure and to the social consequences of these changes.

Per Capita Net Product.[2]   The changes in the productive structure of Latin America in general affected the countries of Groups I and II, generating movement in the net product (Table 5). Modifications in the per capita net product were considerable without being spectacular. With 1950 as a base, the indexes show that in 1963 there was a relatively pronounced variation in these countries, Argentina and Venezuela being the lowest and highest respectively.

The countries experiencing the fastest increases were those less developed in 1950. Argentina, however, which from the beginning of the century—and especially from 1930 on—was partially industrialized, evidences a relative stagnation from 1950 to 1963, whereas countries like Brazil, Colombia, Mexico, and Peru experienced a relatively substantial increase during the thirteen-year period. In Venezuela, oil production contributed substantially to the rise in the net product, causing the high figures in the index and the dollar amount. Since that sector of economic activity was the only one contributing significantly to the net product,[3] Venezuela may be considered a case of fortuitous development.

Even though some of the other countries experienced substantial increases in their product in comparison with Argentina or Venezuela, they are far below the per capita rate of these two countries. Thus, Chile, which in the early fifties also had a product high in comparison with the other countries (except Argentina and Vene-

TABLE 5

EVOLUTION OF PER CAPITA NET PRODUCT IN SELECTED
COUNTRIES OF LATIN AMERICA, 1950–63

	1950		1955		1960		1963	
	$	Index	$	Index	$	Index	$	Index
Argentina	720	100	751	104	788	109	721	101
Brazil	248	100	285	115	322	130	341	137
Colombia	319	100	358	112	378	118	398	125
Chile	393	100	410	104	431	110	462	118
Mexico	249	100	289	116	330	133	344	138
Peru	172	100	198	115	221	128	248	144
Venezuela	870	100	1085	125	1226	141	1257	145

SOURCE: CEPAL. This data was kindly supplied, adjusted, and corrected by P. Orellana, member of the Instituto Latinamericano de Planificación Económica y Social (INSTITUTO).
$ = 1960 U. S. dollars.

zuela), shows a relatively low increase during the period. The increase experienced by Brazil and Mexico is meaningful when we consider that the two countries had a total population of almost 120 million people in 1963. They show a rise in the index figure from 100 in 1950 to 137 and 138, respectively, in 1963. Colombia also experienced an important though less rapid transformation than that of Brazil and Mexico. Peru, which shows a net product lower than any of the other selected countries, has one of the highest rates of increase, about equaling even Venezuela's.

Although there was an increase of per capita net product, probably associated with the rate of industrial development, it is undeniable that both the growth of that product and the industrial impulse, though not insignificant in absolute terms, did not reach figures of any real magnitude on a per capita basis in view of the rapid growth in population in all these countries.

Urbanization.   As indicated by Table 6, the increase of urban population between 1950 and 1960 is perceptible in all seven countries; however, there are peculiarities that should be pointed out. In Chile, and even more so in Argentina, there was already urban predominance before 1950, and the proportional increase of this population merely reinforced a previous condition. In Colombia, Mexico, and Venezuela, the balance in the population swung from rural to urban. In contrast, although Brazil and Peru had a growing urban population, the rural population was still dominant.

TABLE 6

PERCENTAGE OF URBAN POPULATION IN SELECTED
COUNTRIES OF LATIN AMERICA, 1950–60

	Argentina	*Brazil*	*Colombia*	*Chile*	*Mexico*	*Peru*	*Venezuela*
1950	64	31	36	58	46	28	49
1960	68	37	48	66	51[a]	41	61

a. Secretaría de Industria y Comercio VII Censo general de población, Mexico, D.F.

SOURCE: 1950—CEPAL. 1960—Simposio Latinoamericano de Industrialización, p. 32.

THE OCCUPATIONAL STRUCTURE

Table 7 shows trends in the distribution of the employed population according to agricultural and nonagricultural occupations and according to sectors—agriculture (primary), industry (secondary), and services (tertiary). The seven countries fall naturally into two groups: those having more than half of their labor force in farming and those with predominantly nonfarming employment. In 1960 Brazil, Mexico, and Peru were in the first group, and Argentina, Chile, Colombia, and Venezuela in the second. If this trend continues, by 1970 none of these countries will have over 50 percent of farming employment in their occupational structure, and—

TABLE 7

OCCUPATIONAL STRUCTURE OF SELECTED COUNTRIES
OF LATIN AMERICA, 1925–60

(Percentages)

	Argentina			Brazil			Chile		
	1925	1950	1960	1925	1950	1960	1925	1950	1960
Farming	32	24	22	68	61	52	37	30	25
Nonfarming	68	76	78	32	39	48	63	70	75
Manufacturing	(20)	(23)	(21)	(12)	(13)	(13)	(21)	(19)	(17)
Nonmanu-facturing	(48)	(53)	(57)	(20)	(26)	(35)	(42)	(51)	(58)
	100%	100%	100%	100%	100%	100%	100%	100%	100%
	(4,080)[a]	(6,850)	(8,040)	(10,310)	(17,109)	(22,480)	(1,350)	(2,061)	(2,600)

	Colombia			Mexico		
	1925	1950	1960	1925	1950	1960
Farming	65	57	49	70	58	53
Nonfarming	35	43	51	30	42	47
Manufacturing	(17)	(14)	(15)	(11)	(12)	(17)
Nonmanufacturing	(18)	(29)	(36)	(19)	(30)	(30)
	100%	100%	100%	100%	100%	100%
	(2,650)[a]	(4,030)	(5,150)	(5,000)	(8,111)	(11,873)

	Peru			Venezuela		
	1925	1950	1960	1925	1950	1960
Farming	61	59	54	63	42	32
Nonfarming	39	41	46	37	58	68
Manufacturing	(18)	(16)	(15)	(10)	(10)	(12)
Nonmanufacturing	(21)	(25)	(31)	(27)	(48)	(56)
	100%	100%	100%	100%	100%	100%
	(1,750)[a]	(2,788)	(3,490)	(822)	(1,685)	(2,416)

a. In thousands of persons; percentages were extracted from the totals.
SOURCE: Simposio Latinoamericano de Industrialización, pp. 11–13.

even more significantly—in all of them industrial employment will remain proportionally stable, while services will increase substantially. In other words, the agricultural sector will be diminishing in favor of services.

This trend is clear and seems even more marked in countries with greater maturity, such as Argentina and Chile. Therefore, the conclusions of some studies based on isolated analyses of certain countries—studies which emphasize the differences in the effects of industrialization on the occupational structure and on social stratification in underdeveloped countries as compared with developed countries—seem to warrant generalization within the region.[4] Indeed, while in countries of original industrial development the primary sector of the economy diminished initially in favor of the secondary, in Latin America rapid expansion of the tertiary occurs from the very beginning of the industrialization process. Thus the formation of extensive tertiary sectors, which was a late effect of industrialization in Western Europe and the United States, becomes manifest from the beginning of industrialization in Latin America.

Comparative data with regard to the composition of the occupational structure leave no doubts. In Table 8 the Latin American countries in Groups I and II still having more than 50 percent of their population employed in farming by 1960 are compared to countries which were becoming autonomously industrialized during the last century.[5] The fact that in the Latin countries the tertiary sector has expanded more than the secondary indicates that the degree of industrialization achieved is considerably lower than that of the European countries on the respective dates. The results are similar when comparing the Latin countries with an occupational structure of less than 50 percent in farming employment (Table 9). Further, by comparing typical occupational structures of countries of advanced industrialization, such as the United States and Eng-

TABLE 8

OCCUPATIONAL STRUCTURE: THREE LATIN AMERICAN COUNTRIES COMPARED
TO OTHER COUNTRIES AT TIME OF INDUSTRIALIZATION
(Percentages)

	Year	Primary	Secondary	Tertiary
Brazil	1960	52	13	35
Mexico	1960	53	17	30
Peru	1960	54	15	31
Austria	1880	50	28	22
France	1886	52	29	20
Italy	1871	52	34	14
U.S.A.	1880	50	25	25
Ireland	1841	51	34	15

SOURCE: Simposio Latinoamericano de Industrialización, pp. 11–13.

TABLE 9

OCCUPATIONAL STRUCTURE: THREE LATIN AMERICAN COUNTRIES COMPARED
TO OTHER COUNTRIES IN PROCESS OF INDUSTRIALIZATION
AND ALREADY INDUSTRIALIZED
(Percentages)

	Year	Primary	Secondary	Tertiary
Argentina	1960	22	21	57
Chile	1960	25	17	58
Venezuela	1960	32	12	56
France	1954	28	37	35
U.S.A.	1900	38	27	35
Germany	1929	30	41	29
Greece	1940	29	36	35

SOURCE: Simposio Latinoamericano de Industrialización, pp. 11–13.

land (Table 10), and analyzing their evolutionary process, we see
that their occupational profiles are markedly different from those of
Latin American countries with a small primary sector.

The following conclusions become apparent: The proportions between the secondary and tertiary sectors remain more or less equal in the most industrialized countries even though the primary sector is substantially decreased, as in England and the United States, both of which have large tertiary sectors. Expansion of the tertiary sector does not interfere with the expansion of the secondary. Hence, in order to characterize the degree of advancement of the modern-industrial structure of countries like Argentina, Chile, and Venezuela, it would be premature to say that the decrease of the primary sector of these countries points to the growth of the tertiary sector and stabilization of the secondary. Either these countries are developing according to structurally different patterns than those guiding industrialization in industrialized countries, or the data shows that there is "contamination" of relationships between the variables being analyzed. A more detailed analysis is therefore required before making generalizations based on the comparisons.

Indeed, the hypothesis does not appear to explain sufficiently the cause of the characteristic distortion of the urban occupation structure in Latin America; namely, the fact that, with a smaller

TABLE 10

OCCUPATIONAL STRUCTURE OF THE U.S.A. AND ENGLAND,
19TH AND 20TH CENTURIES

(Percentages)

| | U.S.A. | | | England | | |
	1870	*1900*	*1950*	*1881*	*1900*	*1951*
Agriculture	53	38	13	13	9	5
Industry	22	27	37	50	51	49
Services	25	35	50	37	40	46
	100%	100%	100%	100%	100%	100%

SOURCE: Simposio Latinoamericano de Industrialización, p. 11.

percentage of people occupied in the secondary sector industrial production equals that reached by the countries of original development at the time these latter had a primary sector of the same magnitude. The premise of this hypothesis is that industrial development in Latin America is based on modern technological conditions that allow for more production with less labor. This trend is undeniable, as the larger expansion of the industrial product demonstrates when it is compared with the increase of the secondary sector. However, indicators of factors favoring industrialization show that with the present employment distribution in Latin America it is improbable that industrial production equivalent to that achieved by the countries industrialized in the past may be obtained by extension of the secondary sector (see Table 11).

Therefore, available data call for extreme caution in regard to conclusions about the formation in Latin America of a differentiated occupational structure of the type characteristic of the older industrial societies. Does this mean that there have been no significant changes in the ocupational structure, and, hence, when taking the latter as an indicator of social stratification, there has

TABLE 11

PRODUCTION OF ELECTRICAL ENERGY: INSTALLED CAPACITY IN SELECTED
LATIN AMERICAN AND INDUSTRIALIZED COUNTRIES
(Millions of kilowatts)

	U.S.A.	*France*	*Germany*	*England*	*U.S.S.R.*	*Italy*
1928	82,794	12,976	27,870	10,879	5,007	9,630
	Argentina	*Brazil*	*Colombia*	*Chile*	*Mexico*	*Peru*	*Venezuela*
1963	4,584	6,379	1,158	1,136	4,192	1,041	1,977[a]

a. 1962.
SOURCE: 1928—United Nations, *Statistical Yearbook*, 1948, pp. 258–62. 1963—*Ibid.*, 1964, pp. 343–49.

been no formation of "middle strata" nor extension and differentiation of the "popular sector"? The urbanization trends, the formation of the tertiary sector, and the evolution of the industrialization indicators seem to point to the contrary. The Latin American societies considered here have undergone transformation that cannot be underestimated; they have industrialized, but they also present significant differences from the socioeconomic structure of the industrialized countries. Let us analyze this apparent contradiction, using the available data, with the purpose of determining the transformation of the secondary sector and its possible implications in the stratification patterns, and at the same time analyzing the significance of the tertiary sector in Latin America.

Changes in the Secondary Sector

Table 12 clearly shows that the trend of manufacturing employment within the overall nonfarming occupations (secondary and tertiary) is one of proportional decrease. In practically all of the

TABLE 12

PARTICIPATION OF INDUSTRIAL EMPLOYMENT
IN TOTAL NONAGRICULTURAL OCCUPATIONS
(Percentages)

	1925	1940	1950	1960
Argentina	30	32	30	26
Brazil	36	34	33	28
Chile	33	26	26	23
Colombia	48	35	33	29
Mexico	36	32	29	30
Peru	46	41	39	34
Venezuela	27	21	18	18
Latin America	35	33	31	27

SOURCE: Simposio Latinoamericano de Industrialización, p. 14.

more industrialized countries of Latin America, the same pattern is noticeable, which is nothing but the result indicated in Tables 8 and 9: the growth of the tertiary sector at the expense of the primary. Nevertheless, in absolute numbers there is a continuing increase between 1925 and 1960 in the number of persons joining the secondary sector. Thus, the number of people occupied in manufacturing in Argentina practically doubled during these thirty-five years, more than doubled in Brazil, almost tripled in Mexico, and more than tripled in Venezuela; even in Chile, Colombia, and Peru, all of which registered smaller increases, the increase of employment in the secondary amounted to approximately 60 percent. The mass of people moving from agricultural activities to manufacturing is considerable, in spite of the relatively small increase in the secondary sector.

This trend points to a general conclusion, still provisional, emphasizing the numerical importance of the new occupational sectors in the seven Latin American countries considered here. It becomes necessary, therefore, to uncover more details about the new industrial sectors. Let us first analyze changes in the manufacturing sector as presented in Table 13.

In comparing the initial and final dates of this table, it can be seen that only in Peru and Colombia artisan employment continued to be predominate within the overall manufacturing sector. In all other countries the increase of industrial employment surpassed that of artisan employment. It is noteworthy that in Mexico two-thirds of the entire manufacturing occupations belonged to the industrial sector and only one-third to the artisan. Brazil also presents a significant difference that favors industrial employment. In these two countries industrial employment increased six and four times, respectively, during the period of time considered. The data in Table 13 also indicate that differentiation of the industrial sector became accentuated between 1940 and 1950, a period during which

TABLE 13

POPULATION EMPLOYED IN MANUFACTURING SECTOR ACCORDING
TO DISTRIBUTION OF INDUSTRIAL AND ARTISAN EMPLOYMENT
(Percentages)

	1925		1940		1950		1960	
	Ind.	Art.	Ind.	Art.	Ind.	Art.	Ind.	Art.
Argentina	40	60	49	51	61	39	58	42
Brazil	32	68	49	51	52	48	56	44
Chile	29	71	48	52	49	51	54	46
Colombia	11	89	24	76	30	70	34	66
Mexico	30	70	50	50	55	45	64	36
Peru	6	94	16	84	28	71	38	62
Venezuela	14	86	44	56	47	53	60	40
Latin America	26	74	41	59	48	52	52	48

SOURCE: Simposio Latinoamericano de Industrialización, pp. 17–18.

the conditions of the international market favored the intensification of "import substitutions" due to the war.

Table 14 presents data on industrial employment distribution by size of enterprise, data which confirms the importance of the "modern sector" in the occupational structure of the countries considered. With the exception of Venezuela, industrial employment in enterprises of 100 and more workers amounts to 50 percent or more of the total persons occupied in manufacturing; this reinforces the foregoing statements about the importance of the modern industrial sector in employment in manufacturing as a whole. Furthermore, although the secondary sector decreased proportionately in regard to overall employment, the contribution of the manufacturing sector to the formation of the gross domestic product increased in almost all countries (Table 15).

The few data available indicate that in parallel fashion the average remuneration per capita in the manufacturing sector is higher in enterprises of 100 or more workers.[6] All this suggests that relatively better paid strata are formed in the urban-industrial sector.

TABLE 14
PERSONS EMPLOYED IN INDUSTRIAL SECTOR
ACCORDING TO SIZE OF ENTERPRISE
(Percentages)

	1960 Brazil	1963 Colombia	1957 Chile[a]	1961 Venezuela[b]
From 1 to 4 persons	8	4	—	—
From 5 to 19 persons	15	18	15	37
From 20 to 99 persons	21	26	28	26
100 and over	56	52	57	37
	100%	100%	100%	100%
	(1796.8)[c]	(254.1)	(206.7)	(156.9)

a. Data for Chile is not available in the "1 to 4 persons" category.

b. The computations for Venezuela are for 5–20 persons, 21–100, and 101 and over, respectively.

c. In thousands of persons; percentages were extracted from the totals.

SOURCE: Simposio Latinoamericano de Industrialización, p. 35.

TABLE 15
CONTRIBUTION OF MANUFACTURING SECTOR TO GENERATION OF
GROSS DOMESTIC PRODUCT AND EMPLOYMENT IN THAT BRANCH OF ACTIVITY
(Percentages)

	GDP		EAP	
	1951	1960	1951	1960
Argentina	27	32	23	21
Brazil	25[a]	26[a]	13	13
Colombia	14	17	14	15
Chile	19	18	19	17
Mexico	21	23	12	17
Peru	16	19	16	15
Venezuela	8[b]	11[b]	10	12

a. Includes construction, mining and quarrying, electricity, gas, and water.

b. Excludes oil.

SOURCE: GDP—United Nations, *Statistical Bulletin for Latin America,* III, No. 1. EAP—Simposio Latinoamericano de Industrialización, pp. 17–18. Estimates based on official statistics. Data corresponds to 1950 and 1960.

NOTE: GDP has been computed by taking the values at factor cost as a base, except for Mexico, Peru, and Venezuela, whose market prices of 1950, 1960, and 1957, respectively, are used.

These strata—even though they are not considerable in percentage —have sufficient weight in absolute figure to enable one to speak of consolidation of a modern industrial sector having some impact on consumer demand. On the other hand, internal differentiation in the industrial sector is accentuated. Thus, salaries in the "dynamic industries"—which form when the development process turns to the internal market and becomes an imports-substituting process—are noticeably higher than those in the other industrial sectors. At the same time, the number of persons employed in that type of industry has continually increased during recent years.[7] The repercussions of these trends within the manufacturing sector on social stratification are also considerable. Next to a labor sector with a certain capacity for consumption, a sector of technicians and clerks is created that assumes significant proportions within the secondary sector (Table 16).

The conclusions from these data are unequivocal with regard to the effects of the stated structural transformations on the formation and differentiation of the secondary sector. The importance and the composition of the tertiary sector must be analyzed if we are to obtain a clearer idea of the social effects of the transformations.

TABLE 16

MANUFACTURING SECTOR: RATIO OF MANUAL TO NONMANUAL EMPLOYEES
(Percentages)

	Argentina 1954	Brazil 1960	Chile 1957	Mexico 1960	Peru 1960	Venezuela 1961
Workers	70	79	87	65	84	75
Nonworkers[a]	30	21	13	35	16	25

a. Includes employees, family members, and owners.
SOURCE: Simposio Latinoamericano de Industrialización, p. 52.

Changes in the Tertiary Sector

If growth of the tertiary (like that of the secondary) sector had resulted in the creation of occupations directly or indirectly linked

to the impulse of the dynamic-industrial sector, we would be justified in stating that structural changes had reached such a degree in
the socioeconomic structure of Latin America that the concept of
"post-automation industrial societies" would be the only one fit to
describe them. However, this is not the case, as already stated. In
order to have really expressed the differentiation of the urban
services sector, the magnitude of the tertiary sector and its continuing growth would have required a much more developed industrial basis than that actually existing.

As a first approach, the distribution of the tertiary within the
urban sector is given in Table 17. Obviously, the data indicate an
enormous percentage of people in the tertiary sector, compared
with the secondary sector. To explain the phenomenon of an "overloaded tertiary," several hypotheses have been advanced, most of
which express a valid dimension of the problem.

In the first place, the way in which data are usually presented is
inadequate. For example, under the services sector it is customary
to include a series of job classifications ranging from those comple-

TABLE 17

PARTICIPATION OF NONMANUFACTURING EMPLOYMENT IN TOTAL NONFARM
OCCUPATIONS IN SELECTED AND IN ALL LATIN AMERICAN COUNTRIES

(Percentages)

	1925	1940	1950	1960
Argentina	70	68	70	74
Brazil	64	66	67	72
Chile	67	74	74	77
Colombia	52	65	67	71
Mexico	64	68	71	70
Peru	54	59	61	66
Venezuela	73	79	82	82
Latin America	65	67	69	73

SOURCE: Simposio Latinoamericano de Industrialización, p. 13.

mentary to urban industry, such as transport, public service, etc., to those in which underemployment is concealed under sporadic activities of insufficient remuneration. Also, it has been claimed that in the tertiary, bureaucratic occupations assume a disproportionate share. An attempt has been made to explain this rise on the basis of the role of the public service as a channel to absorb the decadent traditional classes. However, information presented in Table 3 indicates that in the overall tertiary sector government employment reaches a moderate increase, from 2.2 percent of the employed population in 1925 to 3.7 percent in 1960. When considering the percentage of this sector in regard to the overall population, the increase ranges from 0.8 to 1.2 percent. Likewise, Table 3 permits a better evaluation of the significance of the tertiary: Some of its items refer directly to occupations related to the growth of the modern sectors of the economy, such as the construction sector or basic services, which registered an increase between 1925 and 1960 from 1.6 to 4.9 percent and from 3.2 to 5.2 percent respectively.

Thus the high tertiary sectors in the developing countries of Latin America, even though they exceed those of countries of original industrialization (and the differences between the patterns of development of the two groups of countries should not be forgotten), express a certain degree of formation of modern urban-industrial strata in the social structure. The difficulty in analyzing the exact significance of that process stems, on the one hand, from the relative indetermination of the marginal sectors within the tertiary sector (formed by the unemployed, underemployed, etc.) and, on the other hand, lies in evaluating the specific weight of white-collar and manual labor activities in the tertiary as a whole.

The information in Table 18, in regard to four of the seven countries being analyzed,[8] refines and clarifies the composition of the tertiary sector. It is very noticeable that in spite of the "normal" and moderate expansion of labor employed in business, finance, transportation, and communications, labor in services increased the most during the same period. Hence, it is possible to consider certain hypotheses that may permit an evaluation of the portion within services that is due to marginalization of urban populations.

Available statistics do not allow an accurate evaluation of the proportion of the unemployed in Latin America, since the phenomenon in most cases is disguised.[9] The presence of unemployment in the tertiary sector is noticeable in the items "miscellaneous services and nonspecified activities." Close to 10 million persons (approximately 15 percent of the labor force) theoretically are engaged in these activities, which have been practically the only items

TABLE 18

PARTICIPATION OF EMPLOYED POPULATION IN TERTIARY SECTOR
(Percentages)

	Argentina		Chile		Mexico		Venezuela	
	1950	1960	1952	1960	1950	1960	1951	1962
Business and finance	11	12	9	9	8	9	9	13
Transportation and communication	6	7	5	6	3	4	3	4
Services (includes governmental, private, and nonspecified occupations	23	28	24	26	15	17	21	26
	40%	47%	38%	41%	26%	30%	33%	43%

SOURCE: Argentina—Simposio Latinoamericano de Industrialización, *El desarrollo industrial de Argentina*, p. 22.

Chile—Simposio . . . , *El desarrollo Industrial de Chile*, p. 14.

Mexico—Secretaría de Industria y Comercio, *VI Censo general de población*, Mexico, 1950; Dirección General de Estadística y Nacional Financiera, Informe de 1961 (for 1960).

registering a decrease in productivity between 1950 and 1960.[10] A wise guess, based on surveys conducted in Chile and Peru, is that in the aforementioned activities there exists approximately 25 percent of "disguised employment." If unemployment existing in business and construction is added to these calculations, the significance of the marginalized population in the urban economic structure can be evaluated more realistically. It is not negligible that in the artisan sector of manufacturing this phenomenon must reach around 15 percent of the employed population, a level equivalent to the estimated rural unemployment.[11] On the basis of these hypotheses it is possible to set up an estimate of the minimal amount of unemployment and disguised unemployment in the countries being studied.

As a provisional consideration, it can be stated that the undeniable differentiation of urban occupation, even though expressing the formation of middle strata, also covers up the existence of marginal masses. When considering the effects of industrialization and modernization on the Latin American economy, we are again confronted with the image of a contradictory movement: the rapid and numerically significant formation of a possible class structure (relatively integrated, dynamic, perhaps open to intensive social mobility simultaneously with the no less accelerated formation of wide social strata apparently not integrated but possibly "available" to the values, institutions and, in a phrase, the "way of life," of industrial society.

SOCIAL STRATIFICATION

In any event, the data presented indicate important changes in the occupational structure of Latin America countries, particularly in the more industrialized countries. It is legitimate, then, to assume there have also been alterations in the social stratification system.

Indeed, the data show that, within the secondary sector, nonlabor groups reached a significant percentage by 1960, and that labor in the industrial category exceeded that in the artisan. As to the tertiary, although it might not be generally considered as an indicator of modernization since nonmanual occupation is usually not considered important in the process of industrialization, the growth in categories such as business or finance leads to the assumption that the nonmanual occupation strata has extended throughout the overall occupational structure.

The analysis in Table 19 of the available data for the employed population as a whole indicates the trends of occupational differentiation. It is necessary to emphasize that urban population strata composed of persons engaged in nonmanual professions (professionals, technicians, scientists, managers, administrators, clerks, and salesmen) assumed a substantial *numerical* magnitude. Again, this phenomenon is more important in theoretical terms than the ratio of nonmanual to overall occupations. Perhaps it is even more important than the growth trends in these occupations, since in some cases the projections disregard the economic changes that occurred between 1950 and 1960. By using the data in Table 19 and ignoring occupations in the "services" and "nonspecified" categories, which are assumed to have a large concentration of marginal groups, it is possible to obtain a relatively realistic image of the occupational stratification of the countries under discussion.

The proportion of nonmanual occupations to manual occupations increased in all countries. In spite of the weakness of the information and the caution required in treating the data, it is possible to construct a simple stratification index indicating the behavior of these two categories (Table 20). The relationship expresses itself much more clearly, of course, when the farming sectors are excluded from the denominator (Table 21). Taken as a whole, the ratio of nonmanual to manual occupations tends to increase, which

TABLE 19

POPULATION BY OCCUPATIONAL GROUPS IN SELECTED LATIN AMERICAN COUNTRIES, 1950–60

(Percentages)

	Colombia[a]		Brazil		Venezuela		Peru	
	1950	1960	1950	1960	1950	1960	1950	1960
Professionals, technicians, and scientists	2	3	2	2	4	4	3	3
Managers and administrators	6	7	5	5	1	1	1	2
Clerks	2	3	3	3	4	8	4	5
Salesmen	2	2	4	4	8	11	5	7
Farmers	53	47	57	57	41	31	51	49
Mining	1	1	1	1	0	1	1	1
Transportation and communication	2	2	3	3	4	7	2	2
Artisans and workers	15	17	13	13	16	19	18	15
Services	11	12	5	5	10	12	7	9
Nonspecified	6	6	7	7	12	6	8	7
	100% (4029.3)[b]	100% (4550.3)	100% (1706.1)	100% (22,341)	100% (1543.4)	100% (2796.0)	100% (2737.8)	100% (3013.8)

a. Projections from the 1950 census. Note that variations exist in the data for Colombia, but not for Brazil. The reason is that for the former additional studies are used that contributed to a refining of the projection, while the latter deals with a "gross" projection.

b. Thousands of persons; percentages were extracted from the totals.

SOURCES: Population census, and CEPAL data. These data were kindly supplied by Marcos Altman, member of the INSTITUTO.

TABLE 20

PERCENTAGE OF EMPLOYED NONMANUALS OVER MANUALS, 1950–60

$$\text{(Stratification index} = \frac{\text{nonmanuals}^a}{\text{manuals}})$$

	Argentina[b]	*Brazil*[d]	*Chile*	*Colombia*[d]	*Mexico*	*Peru*[f]	*Venezuela*
1950[c]	27.8	13.2	20.7	12.3	[e]	[e]	16.3
1960	38.17	15.39	31.27	13.89	24.40	19.29	33.23

a. Nonmanuals includes professionals, technicians, managers and administrators, white-collar workers, and salesmen. Manuals includes farmers, cattlemen, fishermen, lumbermen, miners, drivers (of transports), artisans, domestics, and nonspecified workers.

b. Based on a sample extracted from the census data of 1960.

c. The middle and the lower occupational strata in secondary and tertiary sectors. Data from G. Germani, "Estrategia para estimular la movilidad social" in J. Kahl, ed., *La industrialización en América Latina*, Mexico: Fondo de Cultura, 1965, pp. 274–306.

d. The figures of 1960 are based on projections from the 1950 census (by Marcos Altman).

e. Data not available.

f. It is necessary to note that the Peruvian census includes as "managers" a considerable proportion of individuals occupied in farming who own only a small piece of land. Since some of them are included in the general category of "nonmanuals," the quotient tends to increase.

TABLE 21

PERCENTAGE OF MANUALS OVER NONMANUALS,
URBAN EMPLOYED ONLY, 1960[a]

Argentina	*Brazil*	*Colombia*	*Chile*	*Mexico*	*Peru*	*Venezuela*
51.03	45.22	35.16	[b]	73.01	46.05	56.31

a. See Table 20, note *a*.

b. Data not available.

means that the relative weight of the "intermediate sectors" in the social stratification system tends to increase.

There are relatively few studies from which to draw conclusions regarding the composition of the middle classes and the leading elites (either urban or rural capitalist entrepreneurs). However, there is enough information to construct hypotheses about the orientation, structure, and behavior of these groups. It is now customary to point out the persistence and renovation of the traditional dominating strata, which to a large extent have managed to adapt to the changes of behavior imposed by the development stage based on large-scale exporting of primary products, and, more recently, to face with some effectiveness the changing social conditions of the industrial expansion period based on the internal market.[12] However, the image of a leading class impervious to the upward social flow is no longer a valid one. Recent studies[13] indicate that there is an incorporation of new groups and individuals—administrative or military—into the leading elites, both economically and politically. These studies also indicate a certain "intersectorial mobility" of the elites, which changes function and activity, either passing from the economic level to the political and serving as a means of adapting to economically disadvantageous circumstances for some groups, or changing activity at the economic level, from agriculture to services, from these to industry, to banking, etc., thus securing a certain continuity between the various sectors of the dominating classes and in practice implementing an extensive system of solidarity among the traditional elites and the nouveaux riches.

The flexibility of the traditional leading classes operates in a framework of economic dynamism, as revealed by the data presented in this paper. This dynamism, which is not sufficient to incorporate the whole population into the expanding economic system, does, however, permit upward social mobility sufficient to force the traditional dominating classes to "share command" with the new politically or economically powerful sectors (capitalist entrepreneurs of immigrant origin, technical or professional sectors—mainly the military—of the old or new middle classes, etc.); this dynamism seems capable of creating expectations, fulfilled up to a certain point, of upward social mobility among the popular classes.

The few studies on social mobility in Latin America indicate that the effects of changes in the occupational structure, promoted by economic development, unquestionably permit and to a considerable degree accelerate "structural mobility," as some authors call it—that is, mobility operating through creation of new employment opportunities. However, "replacement mobility," to use Germani's expression, or "position," to use the nomenclature of Hutchinson (mobility due to change of position, disregarding the increase of supply in new higher-ranking employments), appears to be extremely small even in dynamic areas like the city of São Paulo.[14] Hutchinson's study unexpectedly shows that when comparing the results obtained with similar data of a society considered having low fluidity, such as that of Great Britain, the social structure of the city of São Paulo is even more rigid. Once again, therefore, some of the foregoing statements are confirmed indirectly: Industrial development in Latin American countries, although it causes changes in the occupational structure and ultimately in the forms of social stratification, has not resulted in displacing the traditional high social groups to the extent of forming an "open class society." But neither has it allowed the old forms of social stratification and control to remain unaltered: The new social groups, when not displacing the old ones, have acquired upward dynamism sufficiently important to permit some of the new segments to reach the high levels of the stratification system, and to encourage in almost all levels of urban population the hope for upward mobility.[15]

To arrive at a conclusion, the *meaning* of the change process in relation to the type of society forming in Latin America needs to be explored.

ECONOMIC DEVELOPMENT AND SOCIAL CHANGE

The information presented limits the validity of pessimistic interpretations, like those denying the evidence of the existing dynamism in the industrializing Latin American societies, as well as the validity of naïve interpretations establishing an immediate link between the limited achievements of industrialization and economic development and the attainment of social development patterns characteristic of the "mass industrial societies." It would seem, then, that the old concept of a "dual society" would be the intermediate point of balance between the two extreme positions. However, the idea of dual society produces more confusion than clarification.

Indeed, the data and trends presented do not permit the conclusion that two isolated sectors have formed in the societies of the seven countries under consideration: the dynamic, or modern, and the stagnated, or traditional. Actually, it is in what is usually called the urban-modern sector that marginal groups have become established, unincorporated by the dynamics of economic expansion. On the other hand, as has been demonstrated, the new social groups do not completely displace the traditional sectors, and these latter apparently are much more flexible than assumed in commonly held theories on oligarchies.

The impression remains, then, that Latin American societies have experienced changes of some importance, even in rural areas, since (although this aspect was not pointed out in the analysis) the continuing suction of rural populations by the cities alters the traditional equilibrium. The rhythm and direction of the change, however, are not the same for the various sectors of society: Next the pre-industrial society, a policlassist center forms that absorbs part of the new social groups, but a massive population sector forms possibly even faster in its periphery—urban and rural. Its existence is a direct function of the transformation due to expansion of the new economic structure, but the laws governing its movement do not follow entirely the framework of the urban-industrial system. Thus, although it is true that the Latin American "industrialized" societies present two faces, one is a function of the other and not the inverse: The dynamism of the new urban-industrial sector accentuates the growth of the periphery, but this does not mean—in the countries here considered—that the modern policlassist center has ceased to impose its order on the whole society.

The suggested interpretation emphasizes, therefore, that in the social reorganization process a system of alliances arises between the dominating sectors of preindustrial societies and the new high strata formed by industrialization. At the same time, the low strata break up into two different groups: those entering the expanding economic system and those remaining at the periphery. It would seem appropriate in view of the available information to explain in more detail the results of this latter process, pointing out that it is the "modern sector," or "policlassist center" as we choose to call it, that determines the "movement" of industrializing societies, and that the fragmentation of the popular sectors, for the same reason, is relative: Not only does a periphery of society become established in the function of the industrial-capitalist center, but the latter also subordinates the periphery.

The last aspect requires additional clarification. Although the overloaded tertiary and the presence of marginal groups testify to the social consequences of industrialization and the economic system's inability to absorb the excess of labor generated by its operations, the data presented, and some of the studies mentioned in the notes, suggest it would be premature to state that there is a complete rupture between the relatively more integrated core of the social system and the periphery, which many assume to be anomic and "available." In fact, the estimates presented in this paper and some trends in the expansion of the economic system point toward more cautious conclusions, emphasizing that the system in formation has a certain absorption capability and, at any rate, still has many resources to expand the channels of social control, and that the patterns of deferred social upward mobility, even though somewhat mythical, are nonetheless effective.[16]

Otherwise, if common hypotheses about a complete rupture of

the equilibrium between center and periphery or about the inability of the currently-forming capitalist-industrial system to maintain a control system are valid, Latin American "industrialized" societies would already be fully involved in a revolutionary turmoil, which is not the case. On the contrary, situations of this type have come up in countries or regions of Latin America where the impact of industrialization did not succeed in changing the national structure in its entirety, that is, in nonindustrial urban areas. Of course, the need to specify the limits of the absorption capacity of the dynamic economic capitalist sectors and the adaptation forms and reaction of the "mobilized but not integrated masses" remains as a practical problem for the type of future transformation of the region and as a theoretical problem for scientific determination of the type of society that is forming. Due to lack of systematic information on the subject, it is not possible to advance any further than the previous hypotheses; at present it still is relatively safe to talk of the existence of links of the two sectors of the popular classes among themselves and with the policlassist center, as well as of the capacity of this latter to maintain forms of social control by acting on the periphery in a relatively effective way.

Finally, after dismissing the idea of the existence of "dual societies," used to explain the double movement of reorganization of the social system, and after showing that it is economic development that creates a policlassist core and a mass-type periphery at the same time, it should be emphasized that at the center of this type of society differentiation and stratification of the social groups form both an industrial proletariat and a numerically strategic important middle sector. This obviously reflects the existence of active entrepreneurial strata in the private or public sector of the economy. Indeed, if it is true that in society as a whole, rural populations, and those not integrated in many of the countries considered, continue to constitute the majority of the population, the distinctive feature of those societies is precisely the presence of new social groups trying to break into the nation's central society.

It seems, then, that the contradictory movement, which became apparent in the analysis of the specific sectors of the occupational structure of the industrializing countries, attains a general character. The two dimensions of the transformation movement of Latin American societies operate concomitantly in each phase of the development process, and up to now it cannot be foreseen that the process is occurring as a transitional step. On the contrary, the periphery strata increase in absolute numbers, although in the more industrialized countries the differentiation and integration of the groups within the capitalist-industrial system become ever more accentuated. Certainly this process also occurred in the initial phases of European industrialization, but, while in that case emigration and the dynamism of the industrial sector and its capacity to absorb labor seriously decreased the "reserve army," in Latin America industrial societies form in the midst of a periphery of extensive social strata that, if no longer rural-traditional, are not yet truly urban-industrial.

The Latin American situation, in which the capitalist-industrial system develops without disrupting the dependent periphery, cannot be satisfactorily interpreted without pointing out the situation described above. More than a situation of duality, it is a situation of ambiguity: The two processes—reorganization of the class system and formation of extensive social strata dependent on it but weakly linked to it—mold the situation between them, simultaneously and correspondingly. In no way does the resulting amalgam resemble the duality of two polarized situations, one "modern," the other "traditional," or anachronistic. On the contrary, it expresses the way in which it is possible, under the particular condition of underdevelopment and dependency, for Latin American countries to move ahead in their industrialization process.

Notes and References

1. Settlements of over 2,000 inhabitants registered a 55 percent increase during 1950–60, while in the previous decade the rate of increase was 44 percent. Z. Slawinski, "Los cambios estructurales del empleo en al desarrollo de América Latina," *Boletín económico de América Latina*, X, No. 2 (October 1965), p. 161.

2. When analyzing the per capita net product it should be kept in mind that the entire production of all sectors of economic activity are included.

3. In 1962, 1.3 percent of the employed population was occupied by that sector of activity and contributed 31 percent of the total gross domestic product.

4. See G. A. D. Soares, "The New Industrialization and the Brazilian Political System," Santiago: 1966, mimeo. The methodological procedure of that paper was used as reference in analyzing the comparative evolution of the employed population.

5. Colombia is excluded from the table since its employed population is distributed almost equally betwen rural areas and cities.

6. Simposio Latinoamericano de Industrialización, *El proceso de industrialización en América Latina*, Anexo estadístico, Santiago: Comisión Económica para América Latina (CEPAL), 1966, pp. 59–61.

7. *Ibid.*, Table II–18, p. 52.

8. The percentage totals of the tertiary presented here do not coincide with those presented before, since they were taken from national estimates not corrected on the basis of the same criteria as the foregoing.

9. "Disguised unemployment" and "underemployment" refer to the occupations of a very low income level or to situations in which working hours are less than normal. For purposes of analysis, unemployment itself was not considered because of insufficient data. Therefore, the evaluations presented are provisional and probably below the actual level.

10. These statements were taken from Benjamin Hopenhayn, "Occupación y desarrollo económico en Latinoamérica," Santiago: Instituto Latinoamericano de Planificación Económica y Social (INSTITUTO), 1966, p. 17, mimeo. The data are based on that paper.

11. On the basis of those premises, Hopenhayn estimated that as there were a minimum of 8.2 million workers in a condition of disguised unemployment in 1960 (12 percent of the employed population); he estimated that there would be 9.2 million in 1965, and 10.8 million by 1970.

12. For a critical summary of these trends and a bibliography, see F. H. Cardoso, "Entrepreneurial Elites," paper presented at the World Sociological Congress, Evian, September 1966. See also S. M. Lipset, "Elites, Education, and Entrepreneurship in Latin America," paper presented at the International

Seminar on Elite Formation in Latin America, Montevideo, June 1965; and José Medina Echavarría, *Consideraciones sociológicas sobre el desarrollo*, Buenos Aires: Solar/Hachette, 1964.

13. The Instituto Latinamericano de Planificación Económica y Social is carrying out a series of studies on entrepreneurial groups in Argentina, Brazil, and Chile. Partial results obtained from the first of the papers mentioned in the previous note serve as the basis of this statement. See in particular, Luciano Martins, "Deslocamentos intersetoriais na formaçao das elites industriais brasileiras," preliminary discussion paper, and C. Filgueira, "El empresario industrial en Chile," Santiago: INSTITUTO, 1965, manuscript. About the upper classes and the different professional elites, the most significant works are those of José Luis de Imaz; among the most important of his works is *Los que mandan*, Buenos Aires: EUDEBA, 1964.

14. For more details refer to the pioneer studies of Gino Germani and Bertram Hutchinson. The book edited by Kahl (see Table 20, Note *b*) contains a selection, "Movilidad y trabajo," by Hutchinson (pp. 307–36); as to the works of Germani, besides that already mentioned (Table 20), refer to *Política y sociedad en una época de transición*, Buenos Aires: Ed. Paidos, 1962, particularly Chap. 6; also, *Estructura social de la Argentina*, Buenos Aires: Raigal, 1955.

15. It is usually significant that in surveys made of samples of families of the popular class, the objects of social upward mobility are largely the children, for whom a white-collar or liberal profession is generally desired.

16. One of the most significant of the few studies on the behavior of individuals belonging to the "marginal strata" and on their value orientations is that of A. Gurrieri, "Situación y perspectivas de la juventud en una población urbana popular," paper submitted to the Latin American Conference on Children and Youth in National Development, Santiago, November–December 1965.

JOHN P. POWELSON

Toward an Integrated Growth Model:
The Case of Latin America

T WENTY years after the fact, it is beginning to dawn on United States policy-makers—but not on economists—that the "new" economic thought in Latin America is here to stay. For awhile hope was nourished that the theory of deteriorating terms of trade would die down once it had been categorically discredited. Structural inelasticities of supply, the essential balance of payments deficit, the negative foreign investment effect, and the integration of disparate economies—all such theories, it was hoped, were youthful aberrations that maturity and proper guidance would overcome.

But if policy-makers have come to "tolerate" the economic thinking of the South, Northern[1] economists have not. The perusal of recent literature prompts the conclusion that concessions by the

John P. Powelson is Professor of Economics in the University of Colorado.

U.S. State Department and Congress (for example, adherence to the coffee agreement or financial support of integration and inflationary budgets) are purely pragmatic. They do not reflect a conversion of economists to the belief that either the conditions of Latin American development or its goals are fundamentally different from those experienced by the United States.

National schools of economic thought are not new. The "classical" doctrine (Smith, Ricardo, Mill, etc.) is associated with England, and to a lesser extent with France. List and his school are German, and the marginalists are Austrian. But the distinction between previous national schools and the emerging Latin American school is that the former generally proclaimed themselves universal. Though List was influenced by Germany's relative backwardness in relation to England, he nevertheless attacked Smith for omitting nationhood from an essentially boundaryless theory, a concept presumed equally applicable to England. The Latin Americans, on the other hand, do not dispute the appropriateness of classical (or neo-Keynesian) doctrine to the United States. They simply say it does not apply to them.

As a result, they have been labeled bad economists. Northerners are too polite to say so in the literature, but the implication is there. Belief is widespread in the United States that the economic thought emerging in Latin America is sophomoric, unanalytical, and lacking in rigor. It is ideological, hence "soft." Its persistence in spite of theoretical disproof is a cause of wonderment mixed with dismay.

It is the thesis of this paper that the policy conclusions of Latin American economists are often more astute than their economic analyses would imply. The support of Latin American practices by United States policy-makers, furthermore, is more soundly based than might be supposed from our economic doctrines. It follows that it is economic theory that is in the rearguard. But how? And why?

This paper contends that economic growth in the United States has always involved fewer noneconomic variables than it does in Latin America. Political institutions, cultural attitudes, and national consensus have all grown pari passu with technology and capital. This happy circumstance has enabled economists (Domar, for example) to neglect these variables in forging their theories. Nay, more, the conviction has grown that any theory that does include them is soft or ideological; the economist has an axe to grind and his theory cannot therefore be accepted as rigorous.

It is trite to say that the history of Latin America is different from our own; technology and capital have been suddenly thrust upon its countries with no time for the sociological and anthropological variables to catch up. Yet for all its triteness, this fact has never been acknowledged in economists' growth models. It would seem that noneconomic variables should be measured and included as elements in macroeconomic policy. Their inclusion by politicians and exclusion by economists is largely responsible for the lack of prestige of Southern economic theories.

Yet Northern economists share the responsibility, for steeped in our own tradition, we deprecate models that we interpret as soft and ideological. Faced with Northern intransigence, Southern economists have concluded that growth theories based on noneconomic variables will make no headway with their colleagues from the North, and they have allowed this attitude to influence their analyses. As an example, while Northern economists believe that limits to foreign investment lie in a nation's absorptive capacity (a marginal productivity concept), they do not recognize that an even lower limit may be optimum to maximize national identity and consensus ("soft" variables). Therefore, to placate the Northerners, Southern economists have woven theories that admit only "hard" variables ("foreign investment must be limited because it harms the balance of payments"). The result is that their theories do lack rigor, and their reputations decline proportionately.

THE ECONOMIC ARGUMENT

In this section, I shall outline some of the new Latin American economics and indicate in what ways their logic has been disproved in the United States. I shall then turn to the noneconomic variables which, I believe, lend substance to the policy conclusions of Latin American thought, and my conclusion will constitute a plea for an integrated social science model of growth.

Terms of Trade

Latin American economists are most notorious for their argument on the terms of trade. Initially proposed by Prebisch in a United Nations document,[2] the thesis is that over a period of years (Prebisch chose 1876–1938) the terms of trade have been deteriorating for producers of primary products. "With the same amount of primary products," Prebisch argues, "only 63.5 percent of the finished manufactures which could be bought in the 1860's were bought in the 1930's; in other words, an average of 58.6 percent more primary products than in the 1870's are needed to buy the same amounts of finished manufactures."[3]

This conclusion contradicts the probable results designated by classical theory. As productivity increases in manufacturing nations, one would expect them to lower, not raise, their prices in comparison to nations producing primary products. As incomes in manufacturing nations rise, residents may wish to spend a large part of their incomes—but probably not all—on their own products. So long as they prefer to spend any of their higher incomes (however small the portion) on products of primary producers, they will initiate an increase in trade. That is, the manufacturing countries will have to export more than before in order to persuade the primary producers to ship more to them. This persuasion will require a decrease in the price of manufactures in relation to primary products, or, in other words, an *improvement* in the terms of trade for producers of the latter.

That this has not happened, argues Prebisch, is explained by imperfect competition in the manufacturing countries. As productivity is improved, producers have the theoretical choice of reducing prices and keeping wages intact, or of not reducing prices and raising wages. Because of their monopoly positions and the bargaining power of labor, they opt for the latter. Thus the productivity gains, which might have been shared with primary producers through lower prices, are reserved for factors of production in the manufacturing centers. Also, because of the tendency of prices to rise in cyclical upswings and because of their downward rigidity during depressions, Prebisch argues that there is a long-run trend for both wages and prices to increase. Thus the terms of trade not only do not improve for primary producers, they deteriorate.

The thesis has become the whipping boy of Northern economists. Haberler has criticized it as both theoretically invalid and empirically ill-founded.[4] Viner has argued that it fails to take account of changes in the quality of manufactured goods (a pound of copper is always a pound of copper, but a 1967 automobile is far superior to a 1920 model).[5] Others have argued that Prebisch's choice of price indices is biased: It is but a small sample; had he chosen other countries, his results might have been different. Kindleberger, for example, has pointed out that while the terms of trade of underdeveloped countries may have deteriorated with respect to Europe, those of primary producers, taken separately, probably have not.[6]

The most convincing rebuttals of Prebisch have probably been those of Ellsworth, on empirical grounds, and Meier, on theoretical grounds. Prebisch's study was based on the terms of trade of England, with import prices quoted c.i.f. Ellsworth points out that from 1876 to 1905 a sharp decline in transportation rates explains the entire apparent fall in prices paid for many primary products.

While making some concession to the Prebisch theory, he argues that for the remainder of the period declines in the prices of primary products could be explained not by a simple "monopoly" theory but by overproduction and the growth of substitutes, forces that normally ought to be welcomed as indicators that factors of production should move into other, more profitable ventures.[7]

Meier's rebuttal reverts to classical theory, but he explores further, examining the conditions under which increases in productivity might be expected to turn the terms of trade in favor of or against the country initiating the increase.[8] Basing his analysis on reciprocal offer curves, he concludes that any productivity increase causing the innovating country to want to increase either its exports or its imports will turn the terms of trade against it. It would want to increase its exports because—in accordance with classical doctrine —its income has risen and (probably) it does not want to consume its entire increment but would prefer to trade some for the products of other countries. He divides technological innovations into three types: labor-saving, capital-saving, and neutral. The latter reduce the inputs of capital and labor in the same proportion. He then analyzes separately the impact of each of the three on labor-intensive industry and on capital-intensive industry.

Space does not permit a complete recapitulation of Meier's findings, but a few examples will suffice. Suppose the United States specialized in capital-intensive industries that produce for both home consumption and export. There are, however, also labor-intensive industries producing for home consumption which compete with imports. Let us assume a capital-saving innovation in the export industries that causes reduction in costs and expansion of output. There will be pressure to increase exports, which can be satisfied only by a reduction in the barter terms of trade.

Not only that, but there may also be pressure to import. The innovation has saved capital, but any expansion of output will require additional labor. Thus wages will rise in the export sector, and labor will flow from labor-intensive, import-competing industries into exports. The decrease in output of the import-competing industries will increase the demand for imports. Thus the terms of trade will move against the United States not only because of the increased supply of exports, but also because of increased demand for imports.

In similar fashion, Meier analyzes the impact of other types of innovations on the two sectors. In only a few cases does he conclude that the innovating country (say, the United States) would decrease either import demand or export supply. This might occur, for example, with a neutral innovation in the labor-intensive, import-competing sector, which would increase its production (and hence decrease import demand) without necessarily affecting the capital-intensive sector. Taking note of all the possibilities that Meier discusses, however, leads to the conclusion that in most cases, the terms of trade theoretically will move against the innovating country.

Where, then, does the Meier rebuttal confront the Prebisch theory? Meier used *real* reciprocal demand curves, implying that the innovating countries would offer different quantities of exports in exchange for specific quantities of imports, *regardless of internal wage-price policies*. It follows that if their prices did not lead to the offers and demands stipulated by the reciprocal schedules, there would be an offsetting adjustment in the exchange rate. Prebisch apparently forgot about the exchange rate.

For example, suppose the United States produces 100 units of X with 100 hours of labor at a wage of $1 an hour. At zero profit, X sells for $1 a unit, or a total of $100. Now suppose an innovation makes possible the production of 200 units with the same labor input. If output is in fact doubled, there are two extreme wage-price possibilities: Either the price may remain the same ($1) with wages doubled (to $2), or the price may be halved (to $.50) with wages the same ($1). In either case, the real wage of American workers is doubled.

Suppose that before the innovation, Americans had traded 75 X (at $1) for 150 Y (at 2 pesos). To clear the market, the exchange rate would have to be 4 pesos to the dollar. Let us suppose that after the innovation, the intersection of reciprocal offer curves shows that Americans will trade 100 X for 150 Y. If the Americans reduce the price of X to $.50 (and the price of Y remains 2 pesos), then the implied exchange rate becomes 6 pesos to the dollar. If the Americans do not reduce the price (it remains $1, while the price of Y is also unchanged at 2 pesos), then the implied exchange rate becomes 3 pesos to the dollar. In either case, the real exchange ratio is 100 X for 150 Y, and the terms of trade have moved in favor of the peso country. Thus it does not matter whether the innovating country increases wages or reduces prices; the terms of trade depend on the real reciprocal offer curves.

The classical position that offer curves of monopolies are different from those of competitive industries is no defense for the Latin American position, for here we are concerned with the direction of shift (to the left or to the right), not the shape. In less technical terms, we are saying that the extent to which Americans will share the fruits of their technology depends on how badly Americans as a whole want to exchange their increased output for that of foreigners, and not on whether the increment is distributed to Americans through higher wages or lower prices.

If the above reasoning is correct, one might expect Latin American currencies to appreciate over the years with respect to the dollar. They have not done so, not because the theory is wrong, but because internal monetary expansion has depreciated them at a greater rate than they might otherwise have appreciated.

The authors cited have not proved that the terms of trade have not moved against primary producing countries; they did not set out to do so. They have only demonstrated that both the empirical and theoretical bases for the Prebisch argument are not well founded.

Structural Inelasticity of Supply

On first encounter, the term "structural inelasticity of supply" appears redundant to Northern economists; it implies an inelastic inelasticity. The Latin Americans, however, distinguish between supply that is inelastic because of the physical production function (mineral output cannot be increased quickly because of extensive geological explorations and the time required for digging mines) and supply that is inelastic because of the social structure (agricultural output cannot be readily increased under feudalism).

Once the term "structural" is explained, Northern economists are generally willing to accept it. Some may question whether structural inelasticities in Latin America are any greater than they were in the early history of the United States ("the development of the United States seems all too easy now that it is accomplished"), while others, including the present author, are willing to concede that they probably are. The real dichotomy is not in whether there are structural rigidities, but in what may feasibly be done to surmount them.

The structural theory of inflation comes first to mind. The issue has been debated in Latin American journals[9] and in a North American volume edited by Albert Hirschman.[10] The "structuralists" (mainly Latin American) and "monetarists" (some are Latin American, but their institutional dean is the International Monetary Fund) have been set against each other. Yet a survey of the literature reveals that the "monetarists" do not deny the structural causes of inflation. The question of whether inflation is generated by credit creation or evolves from structural considerations is readily resolved. The issues are: How much inflation is to be tolerated? And how are excesses to be controlled?

Here is the place for "bad economics." Northern economists have long "known" that inflation cannot be stopped by more inflation. Plentiful (and painful) experience in Germany, China, Greece, and more recently in Brazil is totally convincing. Not only that, but the theoretical case is compelling (Galbraith even makes the point in *The Affluent Society*[11]). While the structuralists argue that the increased output generated by permissiveness toward inflation will some day overcome the inflation, "more seasoned" Northern economists "know" that inflation will not cease until voluntary saving equals proposed investment, that saving is a function of income (among other things), and that the real income increase necessary to generate a volume of saving sufficient to combat Latin American inflations is enormous. Long before that volume is achieved, the erosive qualities of inflation may well have destroyed the economy.

The "essential" balance of payments deficit is also an outgrowth of structuralist theory. In 1949, the Economic Commission for Latin America (E.C.L.A.) introduced the "capacity to import"[12] (a term not frequently used by Northern economists), measured as the volume index of exports multiplied by the terms of trade. The capacity to import would be impaired if the terms of trade declined more than a proportional amount to an increase in exports. E.C.L.A. then concluded that "as per capita income expands, imports generally tend to rise more than the capacity to import,"[13] thus leading to balance of payments deficits as an essential concomitant of economic development.

Northern economists immediately challenged the concept of the "capacity to import," initially arguing that it did not take into account the imports made possible through foreign investment. E.C.L.A. accommodated them by adjusting its measurement for the inflow of capital minus debt service payments. Even so, in its studies of development prospects of various Latin American countries, it predicted that imports would inevitably outstrip the country's capacity.

This declaration left E.C.L.A. in a vulnerable position. In the first place, the parameters (such as marginal propensity to import) were based on inaccurate and incomplete data whose projections into the future were questionable. In the second place, the theoretical conclusions implied by the capacity to import were not readily accepted by Northerners. E.C.L.A. appeared to support the thesis that structural rigidities (such as the inelastic supply of and demand for primary products) made export expansion difficult, while lack of technical capacity and capital made impossible the growth of import substitutes in sufficient quantity to keep import demand within Latin American capacity. Northern economists, who would more typically attribute Latin America's balance of payments problems to improper fiscal and monetary policies and inappropriate exchange rates, were unconvinced by the E.C.L.A. arguments, which to them lacked rigor. The arguments violate the law of comparative advantage, which to Northern economists is the epitome of rigorous theory, logically proved. The Northern position is best exemplified by the International Monetary Fund, which awards stabilization and exchange policies a higher priority than development planning as a solution to the balance of payments problem.

The law of comparative advantage, in its modern sense, does not imply rigidity of comparative advantage (that Latin America will "forever" be condemned to produce primary products). Rather, it does imply that the transfer problem can be solved, though perhaps at the cost of deteriorating terms of trade. That is, as Latin Americans make the structural changes required by growth (and without which growth is impossible anywhere), a proper exchange policy will induce the growth of exports and import substitutes in such a way that Latin American countries can finance their imports. The deterioration in the terms of trade may arise because, as stated in the Meier argument previously cited, the fruit of technological progress will be shared with other countries. But terms of trade losses will occur simultaneously with rising incomes (that is, *factoral* terms of trade will not deteriorate), which ought to be satisfactory to Latin Americans.

Foreign Investment

The optimum quantity and type of foreign investment is a much debated point, in which Northern economists frequently opt for a greater rate of flow than the Southerners as well as for a higher ratio of private to public capital than the Southerners desire. In fact, Victor Urquidi (of Mexico) reports, that "in the principal countries, except Venezuela, the majority opinion, according to a recent report of an advisory group of the E.C.L.A. and the O.A.S., is rather against than in favor of foreign capital."[14]

The arguments of Northern economists in favor of private investment are too well known to be elaborated here—the capital, technology, training, management expertise, demand, and new products (forward and backward linkages) that accompany private investment. It may surprise some Northerners that Latin American economists question its contribution to their development, and that many agree, along with Urquidi, that public capital (from international lending agencies) is much to be preferred to private.[15]

Latin Americans frequently cite the comparison between inflows of capital and outflows for interest and dividends. For example, Urquidi reports that "the business earnings, interest, and royalties on private foreign capital paid by Latin America represent a sum in excess of annual net investment received."[16] Similar comparisons are implied by E.C.L.A. in its studies of economic development in various countries,[17] where forecasts of investment inflow are set against forecasts of interest and dividend requirements. In 1965 the inflow of capital investment into Mexico was only 180,595 million pesos, while interest and dividends were 234,928 million pesos,[18] a comparison widely commented on in the Mexican press.

Most Northern economists would immediately point out that such comparisons are spurious in assessing the total contribution of foreign investment to the Latin American balance of payments, for they omit the merchandise account. Foreign capital contributes to the balance of payments not only by its own inflow, but also by the exports and import substitutes that emanate from it. In Venezuela the principal contributions of the oil companies to the balance of payments come from the export of oil, not from the inflow of capital. In Mexico, the balance of payments is helped by the radios, refrigerators, automobiles, and other durable goods that do not have to be imported because foreign investment has made possible their production at home. The Chase Manhattan Bank reports: "There are numerous examples of U.S. firms that have reduced the import needs of a country, have created new exports, and have made local firms much more export-minded. U.S. mining affiliates abroad, for example, exported $2.3 billion, or some 80% of their total sales, in 1964. Manufacturing subsidiaries produce mainly for the local markets, but even so, their exports reached $6.7 billion in 1964, some 18% of their total sales."[19]

The most comprehensive approach to the foreign-investment–debt-service problem has probably been that of the Economic Department of the World Bank, as set forth in the volume generally known as the Avramovic study.[20] This study concludes that a problem does exist, in that the percentage increase in income of developing countries may be roughly proportionate to their capital investment (some of which is foreign) and that their marginal propensity to import may be higher than their ability to increase their exports. We are now back at the problem of structural rigidities and "capacity to import," but we become aware that the problem is closely related to that of foreign investment, for debt service is one of the most rigid items in the balance of payments.[21]

Rather than reach the facile conclusion that "foreign investment should be curtailed," the Avramovic study analyzes reasons for high ratios of debt service to exports and proposes certain lines of policy action. Part of the cause lies in improper monetary and fiscal policies that have promoted imports and unwise borrowing to finance them. If these were eliminated and "proper" policies instituted, there would still be a pressure during the early stages of growth. But the Avramovic study reasons that, basically, foreign investment promotes growth: "By making possible a higher rate of investment than would otherwise be feasible, foreign capital raises the rate of income growth."[22] Therefore, the developing country should look forward to the future when investment will have led to a more diversified composition and increased level of exports, which in turn will solve the balance of payments problem.

Apart from the differences in conclusions, a principal distinction between the Southern and Northern approaches (if the Avramovic study may be included in the latter) is once again the more careful analytical nature of the Northern approach and the greater number of hypotheses explored. In general, in the eyes of Northern colleagues, this is the "more scientific approach." As will be shown later, when noneconomic variables are introduced, it does not necessarily follow that the conclusions of Northern economists are superior to those of Southern.

Economic Integration

The question of Latin American integration has been so fraught with North-South controversy, both on a political and intellectual level, that it is hard to decide which of the numerous writings to cite. The classical theory of economic integration, as developed by Viner and other (principally Northern) economists, has traditionally distinguished between benefits and costs of integration, depending on whether integration is primarily trade-diverting or trade-creating. An economic union that causes its members to buy from each other goods formerly produced and consumed in the same country is trade-creating, whereas one that causes them to buy from each other goods that were formerly produced in third countries is trade-diverting. Presumably, costs will be decreased (and hence real incomes increased) in trade creation, but they will be increased (and real incomes decreased) in trade diversion. Thus, if the Latin American Free Trade Area causes, for example, Argentinians to buy in Brazil rather than Argentina, the reason will (presumably) be that the Brazilians can produce cheaper than the Argentinians; hence Argentine incomes will be increased. But if it causes them to buy in Brazil some product that may be more cheaply produced in the United States or Europe, then presumably Brazilian production is more expensive, and Argentine incomes are decreased. These results would follow from the *free choice of buyers* before and after a union is formed.[23]

Contrary to the suppositions of previous writers, Viner concludes that complementary economies (as when country A produces primary products and country B produces manufactured goods) are not such good candidates for integration as competitive economies (where, say, both produce manufactured goods), since trade diversion will be more likely in the former and trade creation more likely in the latter.

Northern economists have frequently argued that Latin American economies are neither complementary nor competitive; they are disparate. "For the most part," writes Kindleberger, "the Asian and Latin American countries have only limited trade among themselves, trading mainly with the countries of Europe or with the United States. Their trade structure, therefore, does not lend itself to an automatic payments arrangement."[24] Southern economists argue, however, that economic integration is a dynamic concept that looks to the future. Trade will be developed and new comparative advantages gained. Thus the law of comparative advantage is not violated, and perhaps because of this, economic integration has received support from many U.S. economists (such as Bela Belassa, Raymond Mikesell, and Sidney Dell).[25] Nevertheless, the works of these economists and others indicate that the Latin American Free Trade Area has not been designed so as to insure its success. Other Northern economists "know" (from the experience of their own countries) that many years are required to change comparative advantages, and that a premature arrangement can do more harm through trade diversion than it does good through the creation of new industries.

The struggle for a Latin American Payments Union brings the dichotomy into clearer focus than does the general question of integration. Southern economists have argued that such a union is necessary because of the persistent dollar shortage.[26] The International Monetary Fund, which has never subscribed to the Latin American doctrine that exchange shortage is structural, has been adamant in insisting that any services that a Latin American Payments Union could possibly render could be done (and are being done) more efficiently and cheaply by the international monetary system (i.e., by banks in New York). The Monetary Fund's great fear, of course, is that Latin Americans (with their "soft" theories on inflation) would automatically grant credits to each other, thus spreading inflations internationally. In 1963 the Fund declared willingness to study the possibility of a payments union provided that automatic credits were eschewed.[27]

Conclusion

The foregoing is not intended to imply that there is a clear line of distinction between Northern and Southern economists, or even that a single economist may not at some time fall in both camps. Rather, our thesis is that there exists a dichotomy between two lines of thought, one of which has its origin and support mainly in Latin America and the other mainly in the United States and Europe. Furthermore, Northern economists tend to regard this Latin American economic thought as inferior for its lack of rigorous analytical content.

In principle, economists (be they Northern or Southern) demand two essentials in a theory. One (the empirical test) is that the theory be statistically demonstrable, with adequate samples if possible, and the other (the theoretical test) is that it be rigorously logical. To many Northern economists, Latin American economic thought fails on both counts. Deteriorating terms of trade have not been demonstrated with adequate samples, and their theoretical justification is based on a fallacy. Though inflation may be attributed (in part) to structural rigidities, there is no example of inflation being solved by more inflation, and the theory of how this will happen has always been loosely argued. The indispensable balance of payments deficit that accompanies development is not really "indispensable," since other countries have developed without it (logically, a single exception is sufficient to disprove a hypothesis). There is some evidence that developing countries now may encounter balance of payments problems, but no evidence that these cannot be overcome with proper monetary and fiscal policies. The thesis that foreign investment is deleterious to a developing country runs counter to all the evidence of history, and the simple comparison of capital inflows with debt service payments is spurious. Finally, the case for economic integration in Latin America conflicts with the theory of trade diversion, a theory which has never been adequately challenged.

Despite my siding with Northern economists on all the above points, I am nevertheless prepared to argue that Latin American policy conclusions based on the above theories are probably consistent with the long-run aims of economic growth of Latin countries. If Southern economic theories lack rigor but their policy conclusions are sound, then it follows that other variables and/or other lines of reasoning—and I propose that these are noneconomic—need to be considered. These are discussed in the following section.

VALUES AND CONSENSUS IN ECONOMIC GROWTH

It has been the history of Europe, the United States, and Canada that a sense of nationhood has grown simultaneously with economic development. This phenomenon has not been characterized only by ethnocentrism, chauvinism, and apartness, faults long condemned by economists. Rather, it has led to a set of dominant values on which national consensus has formed, and this in turn has induced the collaboration of disparate groups of individuals, without which the division of labor would have been impossible.

This dominant set of values consists of values that virtually everyone, with the exception of an easily controllable fringe, accepts as his own. Picture a nation of individuals, each with a set of values. Virtually every individual set of values intersects with every other set of values in a common subset. Furthermore, this common subset is dominant to each individual set of values to the extent that, if any one of the values of the subset conflicts with a value outside the subset, the outside value will be sacrificed and the subset will remain dominant.

Some values in the subset are readily recognized. In the more developed countries, they include the supremacy of law and order, peaceful succession of political office, and the sanctity of contract.

But there are other values as well: an orderly way of doing business, respect for neighbors and colleagues, an accepted relationship between achievement and compensation, obligations of the individual to society (and vice versa), and the like. The important point is that each individual accepts the common values as his own, and that they are dominant. Thus he will not attempt to achieve any personal or regional goal that would destroy them. For example, "everyone ought to pay his taxes" may be one such value. This does not mean that an individual will not cheat if he has the opportunity to do so without (he supposes) destroying the value. It does mean, however, that he will freely vote for social sanctions that make it difficult for him and his neighbors to cheat, that he will aid in their enforcement, and that he would not cheat if he thought that by so doing he would bring down the system. Finally, it is socially unacceptable to cheat, and those who do so successfully do not boast of their achievement.

The greatest contribution of a common subset of dominant values to economic development is that it serves to contain conflicts. For example, shortly after the passage of the Civil Rights Act of 1964 in the United States, a group of newspapermen visited hotels and restaurants in the South to evaluate attitudes on compliance. Although there was some violence and a few establishments closed voluntarily, nevertheless the dominant view expressed was: "Yesterday the law required us to exclude Negroes; today it requires us to serve them." Few were willing to destroy the system of law (a common, dominant value) in order to preserve segregation (a regional value).

Once conflict is contained through a dominant set of values, then it is possible to open one's vista to common interests previously obscured. For example, it is unlikely that labor and management engaged in armed conflict (or indeed, nations at war) will cool their passions sufficiently to observe the goals they have in common. Certainly Bolivian miners and the management of the

Compañía Minera Boliviana have been too busy jailing and hanging each other to philosophize over how their common interests can be served by increased efficiency and higher levels of production.[28]

Economic growth implies conflict. Any increment in the gross national product will bring with it disagreement as to how it should be distributed. Lack of conflict may therefore characterize underdevelopment. Yet sustained growth requires division of labor and hence the collaboration of conflicting groups. The lack of orderly channels for conflict resolution is therefore another characteristic of underdevelopment. Symptoms are hatred, name-calling, the conviction that the goals of one group can be served only through the destruction of those of another, and the formation of ephemeral unions motivated by common enemies rather than lasting unions motivated by singleness of purpose.

How does one forge a set of common, dominant values? How is consensus achieved? These, I propose, are among the most crucial questions of economic development. I will not go so far as to say that they are more important than investment, for the two are on different levels and comparison is meaningless. I do argue, however, that consensus on dominant values is probably a sine qua non and that, to my knowledge, the problem of achieving consensus has been largely ignored by social scientists. Economists have ignored it because it is not one of the variables historically within their domain, and social psychologists (in whose domain it presumably falls) have passed over it because they have not been concerned with economic development. In short, it has been a victim of the compartmentalization of the social sciences. The pity of this is all the greater because such values both form and are formed by economic variables (among others). Indeed, I suggest that here may lie the missing link between the lax Southern economic thought and the intuitively correct policy implications presumably based on it.

Albert Hirschman came close to this view when he suggested that theories might have a "purpose" other than simply to distill principles gained from empirical observation. He distinguished between "privileged" and "neglected" problems, depending on whether they had attracted the attention of policy-makers or not. Parliamentary action on a neglected problem can be stimulated if a theory is forged to link its solution to the solution of a privileged problem. "Sometimes, as in Chile, rather elaborate theories were needed to forge a causal link between the privileged and the stepchild problem, and such theories will frequently have a strong ideological flavor."[29]

Liberal economists in a classical world have always considered nationalism a negative factor. At least, Smith has dominated List in the Anglo-American thought that pervaded the western hemisphere before the Latin Americans challenged it. The division of the world into nations has presumably impeded the maximization of incomes under comparative advantage and the international mobility of factors of production. This view is so well entrenched among Northern economists and policy-makers that almost nothing can shake it. Few, if any, United States ambassadors and foreign service officers think that the purchase of North American investment by Chileans and Mexicans promotes their economic growth. In a decision based entirely on economic variables, most conclude that such purchases constitute a capricious export—from less developed to more developed countries—of capital that would better serve development at home.

Why, then, do the governments of Latin America show such antipathy to foreign investment? There are, of course, some groups (such as domestic businessmen competing with foreigners) that stand to gain economically from a negative attitude toward foreign investment. But to suppose that these have a dominant voice in policy (a view sometimes held) or that, with silver tongues, they have persuaded policy-makers that what benefits them benefits the nation is, I believe, a gross exaggeration. Rather, I suggest that there is intuitive acceptance among development-minded politicians of Latin America that nationalism is the key to forging a common subset of dominant values, that the long-run contribution of this subset to economic growth will be greater than the foreign capital thus displaced, and that its displacement is a necessary ingredient to nationalism.

Here, then, is an illustration of interlacing sociological and economic forces in an area long neglected by both sociologist and economist. I offer no theory, but I suggest—as a field for future investigation—that sociologists might find a measurable and causal link between a country's degree of nationalism and its capacity to create a subset of dominant values, and that economists armed with these data in turn might find a relationship between the values and the rate of growth in the gross national product.

Furthermore, the optimum amount of foreign investment for a growing nation could then be projected in an equilibrium function that would include nationalism both as a dependent variable (whose partial derivative would be taken with respect to foreign invest-ment, literacy, education, promotion of interest in politics, and all other forces that encourage or discourage nationalism, and as an independent variable affecting the containment of conflict (which would in turn promote economic growth). It would then no longer be "necessary" for Southern economists to offer the implausible hypothesis that foreign investment by itself harms a nation's balance of payments.

Nationalism in Mexico has been studied by political scientists as an interesting problem per se. North Americans have often marveled at a campaign undertaken by a presidential candidate who knows in advance that he will be elected, yet carried out with all the vigor of a whistle-stop quest for the marginal votes that might, for a politician in the United States, spell victory. Yet no one (to my knowledge) has attempted to evaluate the "sense of being Mexican" that is inculcated into peasants who participate in the political process, and the relationship between this sense and internal migration, literacy, skills, and other factors affecting economic growth.

Let us now turn to the Prebisch argument concerning the terms of trade. Long discredited in the eyes of Northern economists, this theory carries widespread prestige in Latin America. Why? Some might crassly suppose it is a plot by the less developed world to gain a commercial advantage from more developed countries greater than they "deserve" under the laws of the market. Lest we become involved in the moral question of whether market prices are "just" prices, let us instead explore the nature of capital flows from more to less developed countries, with a past-present comparison that they may bear on the question. Consider the following points.

1. Higher prices for exports would increase income in Latin America and therefore presumably contribute to saving and capital formation.

2. Latin America is greatly in need of capital. Though investment is not the sole determinant of output, nevertheless the experience of oil countries (such as Venezuela) shows it is strategic.

3. During the industrial revolution in Britain and in the early days of the United States, private capital was available at rates of interest considerably lower than those now available in less developed countries. No one spoke of "capital shortage" then.

4. One of the reasons for high interest rates in less developed countries today may well be the risk of government instability. If so, there is a vicious circle here—in that the difficulty of capitalization has a bearing on the government's capacity for stability.

5. In contrast to the experience of the United States, foreign capital has long entered Latin America on terms that discourage nationalism. In the United States, the nationality and cultural characteristics of debtor and creditor were closer than is currently the

case in Latin America, where a debtor-creditor dualism has succeeded in separating the bulk of Latin Americans from the "investment sector." Political considerations in the United States have long influenced the flow of both private and public capital; private investment as a "stabilizing force" was encouraged by the Department of State long before the quest for stability was written into the foreign aid program.

6. The political nature of capital through foreign aid is obvious. What is not so obvious is whether the goals of aid to promote economic growth are consistent with political goals of aid. Stressing capital, technology, and the economic "unity" of peoples handed down by classical doctrine, Northern economists have taken this consistency for granted. Groping for an identifiable set of values, Southern economists have not.

Considering all the above, it is not unreasonable to conclude that the "theory" of deteriorating terms of trade constitutes a quest for free and unfettered capital inflows. Since Northerners are unimpressed by its economic "logic," I suggest that the case for commodity agreements could be more impressively made within an integrated social science model that would distinguish the efficiency of various types of foreign investment according to their terms and methods. It is not now fashionable for "capital-output ratio-ers" to make such a distinction, for to them capital is capital, and its origins are not a consideration.

The theory of inflation is susceptible to an analogous interpretation. Here the integrated social science model must take account not only of the narrow question of whether monetary stability promotes economic growth, but whether in the long run stability arrived at in one way is any different from stability arrived at in another.

Mexico and Bolivia form interesting contrasts. Though it is by no means proposed that the different rates of growth in the two countries depend solely on the means by which they achieved stabilization, nevertheless the fact that the Mexicans thought of it themselves (in 1954), while the Bolivians (since 1956) have required repeated exhortations and threats by both the United States and the International Monetary Fund to bear it in mind may be significant.

In their theories of inflation, the structuralist and monetarist are strikingly similar. Both recognize structural factors as causes, and they agree that inflation can be stopped by monetary policy. Differences between their supporters therefore lie in policy. The structuralists argue that inflation stopped by a strict stabilization program may suppress economic growth.

Judged by rigorous economic logic, they are wrong. But when the stabilization is deemed an imposition from the outside, one that impairs the sense of national dignity and the quest for commonly held values, they may in the long run be right. No one has ever demonstrated that a stabilization program sponsored by the International Monetary Fund has succeeded in the long run, judged by both its ability to survive and its contribution to the nation's growth. Is the most recent stabilization program in Brazil, for example, more durable because it occurred largely as a result of Brazilian initiative after earlier withdrawal by the Fund?

My observations on Latin American economic integration derive directly from the above. Arguments over trade diversion and trade creation are peripheral; they are attempts to cast into an economic mold a problem that is essentially noneconomic. The search for consensus on values need not be confined to the national level. Indeed, the economic considerations are such that the search must be extended to a pan-Latin American arena. Decision on a Latin American Payments Union should have nothing to do with the alleged dollar shortage. For reasons of Latin American nationalism, the banks of the area should expand their foreign departments and perform services now rendered in New York.

Finally, the question of exporting inflation through a credit-extending payments union is not solely economic. I join the Fund in fearing that it would happen, but I believe its likelihood would be diminished in time by the growing politico-economic maturity of the surplus countries. There are already countries in Latin America with a vested interest in growth accompanied by stability—Mexico and Venezuela, for example. If these countries, rather than the International Monetary Fund, should sway their neighbors, the contribution to a Latin American sense of identity would be great indeed.

CONCLUSION

Largely because of the traditional compartmentalization of the social and behavioral sciences, it has become customary for both Northern and Southern economists to confine their models of economic growth to economic variables. In general, such models have been satisfactory in explaining the growth of the United States and Europe, where the requisite political and cultural determinants of growth have probably maintained some stable linear relationship to economic parameters. They are unsatisfactory, however, in explaining growth in Latin America.

Attempts to integrate economics with social sciences have generally met with failure, partly because the legitimate scope for such integration has heretofore not been wide in the United States and partly because integrators have presented their proposition with a lack of rigor. Often they have been associated with ideology or with "theories with a purpose."

Latin American economists have recognized that Northern growth theory is not strictly applicable to them. Partly because of the reluctance of Northern economists to admit the existence of noneconomic (presumably "soft") variables, Southern economists have perceived that economic arguments based on such variables will make no headway in international conferences. Therefore, they have forged a set of economic theories (sometimes known as "doctrines") designed to justify conclusions reached intuitively. However, these theorists have been discredited in Northern circles, and their net effect has probably been negative in achieving Latin American goals. Any concessions by Northern economists to Southern viewpoints are due to pragmatic or political considerations rather than persuasion.

A possible resolution of the dilemma lies in an integrated social science model of economic growth. This paper offers no such model, but it suggests a possible relationship between a set of dominant values on which there is national consensus and the rate of economic growth. If this relationship exists, it might form one part of the integrated model. Such a set of values would limit the arena of possible conflict, and by compelling groups to collaborate it would open vistas of common interest that are otherwise obscured. It would both affect and be affected by the quality of labor, the organization of markets, and many other variables now confined to strictly economic models.

Perhaps such a set of values is the missing link that would lend credence to the policy conclusions of Southern economists. While their theories are wrong, their judgments may be right.

Notes and References

1. The terms "Southern" and "Northern" economists are used here to distinguish between those who, whatever their geographic origin, hold to certain economic doctrines whose *support* comes primarily from economists in Latin America or from economists in the United States, respectively. The distinction is a bad one, but pragmatic.

2. United Nations, Economic Commission for Latin America, *The Economic Development of Latin America and its Principal Problems* (E/CN/12/89/Rev. 1), 1950.

3. *Ibid.*, p. 8.

4. Gottfried Haberler, "International Trade and Economic Development," National Bank of Egypt, Fiftieth Anniversary Commemorative Lectures, Cairo, 1959.

5. Jacob Viner, *International Trade and Economic Development,* Glencoe, Ill.: Free Press, 1952, p. 143.

6. Charles P. Kindleberger, *The Terms of Trade,* New York: Wiley, 1956.

7. P. T. Ellsworth, "The Terms of Trade between Primary Producing and Industrial Countries," *Inter-American Economic Affairs,* Summer 1956, pp. 47–65.

8. Gerald M. Meier, *The International Economics of Development,* New York: Harper and Row, 1968, Chap. 3.

9. See, for example, in *Trimestre económico,* the following articles: Herman Max, "El mito de la estabilización monetaria," January–March 1964; Aldo Ferrer, "Reflexiones acerca de la política de estabilización en la Argentina," October–December 1963; Osvaldo Sunkel, "El fracaso de las políticas de estabilización en el contexto del proceso de desarrollo latinoamericano," October–December 1963; Joseph Grunwald, "La escuela estructuralista, estabilización de precios y desarrollo económico; el caso chileno," July–September 1961.

10. Albert O. Hirschman, ed., *Latin American Issues,* New York: Twentieth Century Fund, 1961, pp. 69–125.

11. Boston: Houghton Mifflin, 1958, p. 215.

12. United Nations, Economic Survey of Latin America, 1949, p. 15.

13. United Nations, *Analyses and Projections of Economic Development: I—An Introduction to the Technique of Programming* (E/CN/12/363), June 1955, p. 15.

14. Report of the Consultant Group ECLA/OAS, p. 18; cited in Victor Urquidi, *The Challenge of Development in Latin America,* New York: Praeger, 1964, p. 56.

15. *Ibid.,* pp. 56–58.

16. *Ibid.,* p. 50.

17. See, for example, United Nations, *Analyses and Projections of Economic Development: III. The Economic Development of Colombia, 1957,* (E/CN/12/365/Rev. 1), November 1956.

18. Banco de Mexico, *Informe anual,* 1965, p. 99.

19. *World Business,* November 1966, p. 7.

20. Dragoslav Avramovic *et al., Economic Growth and External Debt,* Baltimore, Johns Hopkins Press, 1964.

21. The Avramovic study argues that debt service is rigid because (1) interest payments are inflexible, and (2) dividend payments will fluctuate with exports only in the export industries; increasingly, foreign investment

in developing countries is supplying industries for domestic consumption, whose output (and profits) do not necessarily fluctuate with exports.

22. *Ibid.*, p. 10.

23. Jacob Viner, *The Customs Union Issue,* New York: Carnegie Endowment for International Peace, 1950.

24. Charles P. Kindleberger, *International Economics,* 3d ed., Homewood, Ill.: Richard D. Irwin, 1963, p. 613.

25. Bela Belassa, *Economic Development and Integration,* Mexico: Centro de Estudios Monetarios Latinoamericanos, 1965; Raymond F. Mikesell, "The Movement Toward Regional Trading Groups in Latin America," in Hirschman, pp. 125–51; Sidney Dell, *A Latin American Common Market?,* New York: Oxford University Press, 1966.

26. See, for example, Miguel Wionczek, *Latin American Economic Integration,* New York: Praeger, 1966, pp. 89–90.

27. Wionczek, p. 89.

28. The often discouraging search for a common set of dominant values by the principal industrial nations, the lack of which not only impedes worldwide division of labor but also makes war possible, is a complete international analogy to the national problems of underdeveloped countries.

29. Albert O. Hirschman, *Journeys Toward Progress,* New York: Twentieth Century Fund, 1963, p. 231. Hirschman used agrarian reform (a neglected problem) and the balance of payments deficit (a privileged problem) in Colombia as illustrations. Only when it was shown that a solution to the agrarian problem would assist (through agricultural exports) in the balance of payments problem were politicians convinced of its necessity.

DWIGHT S. BROTHERS

Private Foreign Investment in Latin America: Some Implications for the Alliance for Progress

MOST Latin American intellectuals, politicians, and businessmen believe that the economic problems confronting the United States and Latin American countries are of a different nature. Consequently, they commonly reject economic theories accepted in the United States, as well as policy based on these theories, as a guide for solving their problems. While it cannot be said that a common viewpoint prevails in Latin America (clearly pronounced differences exist within and between the various countries), there are some common ideas in contemporary Latin American economic thought and policy; thus generalizations are not unwarranted.

At the ideological level, the characteristic viewpoint is nationalistic; the preferred locus of economic power is the state; and, there

Dwight S. Brothers is Lecturer and Member of the Faculty at the Graduate School of Business Administration, and Associate Director of the Development Advisory Service of the Center for International Affairs, Harvard University.

is widespread apprehension of foreign domination and exploitation —especially by the United States. A proposition which is generally accepted is that gains from foreign trade and investment accrue largely to the advanced industrialized countries; and, it is commonly believed that development is inhibited by various structural rigidities, bottlenecks, vicious circles, or what have you, that cannot be corrected by relying on market forces. Also much in evidence are attempts to promote industrialization by means of protection and other types of state encouragement, to substitute domestic production for manufactured imports while reducing dependence on traditional exports of agricultural products and other raw materials, and, in general, to achieve greater freedom from foreign exchange constraints without increasing traditional forms of foreign trade and investment.

These ideas and policies do not prevail without challenge and dissent both from within and outside Latin American countries. Opposing arguments are usually based on the cosmopolitan viewpoint embodied in orthodox, neoclassical economic theory, on assumptions regarding the universal validity of marginal principles as criteria of efficiency, and on appeals to the coordinating, rationalizing influence of market-determined prices and costs. More specifically, the orthodox critique of nationalistic economic theories and policies characteristically found in Latin America maintains: first, that there is neither any a priori reason why the gains from international trade and investment should accrue disproportionately to the advanced countries nor any conclusive evidence that they do; and, second, that promotion of industrialization by protectionist measures and controls imposed on international capital movements are not necessarily the most desirable policies. In fact, the historical record reveals numerous instances in which such measures have resulted in uneconomic, wasteful expenditures of scarce resources and the willful sacrifice of increases in consumption and capital formation that would have been possible otherwise. From the cosmopolitan, neoclassical viewpoint, the nationalist preference for autarky prevailing in Latin America reflects unfounded and costly bias rather than theoretically sound analysis and valid historical interpretation and constitutes a source of substantial drag on national and regional economic development.

IMPORT SUBSTITUTION

These differences in viewpoint are perhaps best illustrated by contrasting development policies based on promotion of exports in accordance with the doctrine of comparative advantage, and import substitution policies directed toward establishment of national industries capable of satisfying demand in the internal market. The issue in essence is whether economic development is best promoted by allocation of productive resources in accordance with national and international market forces or by resource allocation as dictated by governmental policies directed to the goal of industrialization and substantial national self-sufficiency. The orthodox case for market-directed specialization is, of course, that the use of available resources for the production of those goods and services produced with the greatest relative efficiency, and the exchange of part of the output for that of other countries concentrating their production along lines consistent with their own resource endowments, is the most rational pursuit of national self-interest. The conclusion follows that well-functioning national markets and free international trade provide the best means for increasing the volume of goods and services available to a particular country (and perhaps a greater variety and better quality as well), and this in harmony rather than in conflict with the interests of other countries.

The counter argument employed to justify protectionist and other schemes designed to foster self-sufficiency and, especially, industrialization is based on a less elegant, eclectic theoretical foundation, but this argument adds up to an impressive case for the position that the doctrine of comparative advantage is inappropriate as a policy guide for Latin American economies. The basic argument is that neither the national markets for factors of production, nor the international markets for goods and services, operate sufficiently well, and that therefore both domestic and international market forces must be modified by governmental intervention designed to prevent or otherwise overcome various fundamental impediments to economic development. The main points, in addition to those stemming from the well-established argument concerning infant industry (and other closely related propositions based on differences between private and social costs and benefits), are the following: that the instability of the prices of primary products in world markets is a source of serious difficulties for countries specializing in exporting them; that this disadvantage is compounded by a supposed secular deterioration in the terms on which primary products are traded for manufactured goods; that productivity and productivity gains per worker tend to be lower in agriculture and mining than in industrial activities; and, that specialized productive structures are especially vulnerable to the risk of technological obsolescence.[1]

Neither side in the debate has been able to overwhelm the other despite the massive flow of literature and oratory generated over the past fifteen years or so. But because the proponents of import-substituting industrialization have prevailed in the policy councils of most Latin American countries, the practical problem has become that of measuring the relative benefits and costs of this particular development strategy, and setting limits to its application.

Once adopted and vigorously implemented, a national policy of import substitution has the effect of modifying the domestic terms of trade in favor of protected industries to the disadvantage of producers of agricultural and other primary products not similarly favored by government intervention. The industrial sector benefits from relatively rapid growth initially. However, further industrialization is soon limited by the size of the domestic market. This limitation can be overcome if economies of scale and other factors governing production costs permit a degree of efficiency that is internationally competitive before the domestic demand is satisfied. Unfortunately, the scope of the domestic market is often limited by the relatively high cost of domestically produced industrial products and by the lack of income increases in the agricultural and export sectors.

This is the stage in the process that a number of the Latin American countries are now approaching, and as a result there is a gradually developing awareness that further reliance on import substitution as a development strategy is limited. In simplest terms, the restricting factors consist of (1) industrial inefficiency because of inappropriate subsidization in the first place or insufficient attention to efficiency; (2) limited purchasing power in the agricultural and export sectors because of disadvantages imposed by domestic policies or adverse developments in world markets; (3) chronic shortage of foreign exchange, possibly associated with inflation and currency depreciation; and (4) difficulty in achieving a sufficiently high rate of capital formation because of a deficiency in domestic savings or limited access to foreign capital on satisfactory terms.

Under these circumstances a major policy dilemma is now emerging in various Latin American countries: whether to abandon import substitution and the goal of industrialization via protectionism altogether, or to continue along this line while searching for the means for coping with the difficult problems caused by import substitution. If the latter choice in favor of continued subsidization of industrialization is to be made (as it almost surely will be in most countries, if only to avoid the very serious problems of re-adjustment of the structure of production which would otherwise be required), some combination of the following will be necessary: (1) greater attention to the efficiency of protected industries and to the establishment of efficient domestic suppliers of raw materials and manufactured inputs; (2) more emphasis on increasing the productivity and purchasing power of the agricultural sector with the purpose of broadening the domestic market for industrial products as well as reducing costs of food and raw materials for domestic consumption and export; (3) increased efforts to develop export markets for both traditional commodities and manufactures in advanced countries and within regional customs unions; and, (4) discovery of some economically defensible and politically feasible middle ground between the "monetarist" and "structuralist" financial policy prescriptions[2] consistent with the amount and type of capital formation (both that financed by domestic savings and that financed by foreign loans and investments) necessary to achieve the other requirements listed above. In sum, while there are numerous possible avenues of escape from the inherent limitations of the import substitution strategy of development, the difficulties in moving along any of these (and especially along several simultaneously) are severe in most Latin American environments.

SUBSTITUTION FOR PRIVATE FOREIGN CAPITAL

The foregoing brief review of differences concerning what constitutes appropriate policies in international trade and of problems encountered as a result of import substitution has special relevance to understanding the factors governing direct private foreign investment. First, differences of opinion with regard to the relevance of the doctrine of comparative advantage are roughly similar to those which have developed between protagonists and antagonists of private foreign investment—as one would expect, since disagreement in both cases is rooted in the same fundamental quarrel. Thus, understanding the former assists in comprehending the latter. Second, questions raised regarding the role of private foreign investment in Latin American development are necessarily closely akin to those encountered in discussions of the role of international trade, since international movements of private capital are in reality but a special case of international trade. Third, such investment is often motivated by the desire to overcome trade restrictions and, furthermore, it is by means of trade restrictions (and related schemes of import licensing and exchange control) that host countries often attempt to exercise the desired degree of restraint over private foreign investment.

It is not surprising, therefore, to find that Latin American countries which rely heavily on import substitution as a development strategy also (and usually somewhat later) adopt policies designed to restrict the scope afforded private foreign investment. The same nationalistic and theoretical predilections underlie attempts to devise substitutes for private foreign investment that motivate reliance on import substitution—although specific arguments and counterarguments as to what constitutes an appropriate role for private foreign investment are uniquely tailored to the case being advocated. In the remainder of this essay we shall summarize the various objections to heavy dependence on private foreign investment, suggest an agenda for research into the numerous disputed points at issue, and indicate some implications of Latin American attitudes and policies toward private foreign investment for United States policy under the Alliance for Progress.

ROLE OF PRIVATE FOREIGN INVESTMENT

Let us begin by summarizing the orthodox, neoclassical theory of the role of international capital movements in the development process (as distinct from the balance of payments adjustment process). The theory is based on the proposition that allocation of capital is not optimal until marginal productivity is equalized throughout the area under consideration, e.g., the world or the western hemisphere. Flows of capital from the capital-rich countries, in which the marginal productivity of capital is presumed to be relatively lower, to the capital-poor countries, in which the marginal productivity of capital is presumed to be relatively higher, are capable of producing a surplus in the form of increased real product available for sharing by the capital-exporting and capital-importing countries. Free international capital movement is favored for essentially the same reasons as free international trade in goods and services (or, for that matter, free domestic trade): It permits achievement of a preferable position, or realization of a "surplus," for both buyer and seller.

In more specific terms, the flow of capital from an advanced, capital-rich country to a less developed, capital-poor country permits movement of real resources from the one to the other equal to the amount of the capital flow (measured in financial terms) to the recipient country. Leaving aside the intricacies of the transfer process (and the difficulties that may arise from such factors as incompatible consumption and savings propensities, import and export income elasticities, etc.), the recipient country can be assumed to achieve command of the goods and services counterpart of the capital flow. Furthermore, where the foreign investment involves ownership and management by foreign enterpreneurs—i.e., takes the form of direct private investment—additional benefits in the form of technology, managerial skill, and similar intangibles are transferred in some degree from the capital-exporting to the capital-importing country. The recipient country is enriched not only by the goods and services transferred to it, but also because the productive efficiency of these things (and perhaps also that of the existing and future capital stock of the country) tends to be augmented as a result of the intangibles thought to be inherent in direct private foreign investment. Thus, while foreign investors are motivated by the prospect of profits, since such profits must be generated from the productivity of the investment, and since overall output is increased by more than the amounts returned to investors, the recipient country allegedly cannot help but be benefited by the importation of private foreign capital.[4]

Bases of Latin American Attitudes

What forms does the dissent from these simple, orthodox propositions take? There are a variety, to be sure, so that it is difficult to generalize beyond the statement that the characteristic Latin American attitude toward dependence on private foreign financing is antagonistic. But the bases of this antagonism can be classified into three categories: (1) fears derived from, in some degree at least, historical interpretations based on the various theories of imperialist exploitation and domination; (2) objections based on economic and statistical analyses of past experiences and contemporary circumstances attributable to private foreign investment; and, (3) political problems raised within the recipient country by the presence of foreign indebtedness and/or as a result of pressures exerted by private foreign investors and other foreign creditors.

Fear of Imperialism.   The fear of imperialism, in the sense of economic penetration for political purposes, is very real in Latin America and is not entirely unfounded. In order to understand Latin attitudes in this connection, one needs to review the history of Latin American economic and political relations with advanced, industrial countries, as well as the economic and political theories from which the imperialist interpretations of this record are derived. Opposition to economic imperialism reflects, first of all, a strong anticapitalist bias, and, secondly, the obsessions of peoples who, for whatever reasons, have been slow to achieve self-generating economic development and whose freedom of political maneuver at both the national and international level has consequently been constrained. The classical theory of imperialism (which is largely attributable to John A. Hobson's dispassionate Keynesian-type analysis of nineteenth century capitalism rather than to Marxist-Leninist metaphysics) is premised on the idea that the relatively advanced capitalist countries must inevitably become involved in adventures in the lesser developed countries in order to satisfy vital economic compulsions—with the result that the development of these poorer countries is frustrated by foreign economic exploitation and political domination, carried out if necessary by repressive measures, including the use of military force. The theory calls for the formation of an unholy alliance between commercial interests and government officials in the advanced countries, which, regardless of whether economic penetration is viewed as the vehicle for political intervention or vice versa, leads to the victimization of the poorer countries and gives rise to the danger of wars between the advanced imperialist powers as they pursue their respective imperial designs.

We need not delve into the internal logic of the theory nor into the validity of the basic assumptions and the accuracy of the empirical evidence commonly employed to support it—although it should be noted in passing that a glaring omission in the literature is examination of the threat that economic and political imperialism of a socialist variety may also pose for the weaker countries. The point we wish to emphasize here, however, is that United States businessmen and public officials often display a distressing naïveté in these matters, with the result that they unwittingly conduct themselves in the way that those indoctrinated with the theory of economic imperialism expect them to. And the propensity to interpret the actions of United States business interests and the policies of the United States government in terms of classical imperialism is very strong indeed throughout all of Latin America.[6]

It is clear that fear of economic exploitation and external political domination is in large part the product of the historical experience of the various Latin countries. To recount all unwanted foreign interventions in any detail would fill a book, and even to compile a complete listing of unpleasant episodes in United States–Latin American relations would require substantial research and several pages. So let us be selective and brief.

Penetration from Europe began, of course, with the Spanish conquest, which effectively destroyed the established civilizations, substituting unconscionable economic exploitation and despotic political repression. During the colonial period economic contacts with outsiders other than the established colonial powers were virtually prohibited. In the early nineteenth century, when "independence" was substituted for colonial status, European commercial interests and venture capital, usually supported by governments either beforehand or subsequently, were attracted to the area, so that much of the "modern" nontraditional types of economic activity were initially financed by foreign capital and managed by resident aliens. European investors often joined forces with the ruling national oligarchies, but the power of mother countries was relied upon for ultimate protection and support in the enforcement of claims. It is acknowledged by objective historians that these claims were often contrived, rooted in fraudulent practices, and patently unfair to the host countries, and that diplomatic intercession or armed intervention by the European powers on behalf of private investors, while disguised as attempts to achieve legitimate redress for financial injury, were often part of a design to maintain or reestablish European political hegemony in Latin America. Intervention was often motivated by geopolitical designs and balance of power considerations of a sort consistent with the classical theory of imperialism.

Since the last decades of the nineteenth century, foreign investment and political and military interventions in Latin America have emanated principally from the United States. At first these interventions were cloaked in the mystique of the Monroe Doctrine[7] (i.e., were ostensibly in defense of Latin Americans against European domination), but subsequently the justification came to rest upon United States economic interests (e.g., requirements for raw materials and for export markets) and national defense considerations (e.g., the desirability of preventing hostile regimes being established in strategically sensitive areas). Certainly the record of United States interventions in Cuba and Mexico before World War I, in Santo Domingo and Puerto Rico between the two World Wars, and in Guatemala, Cuba, Brazil, and the Dominican Republic in recent years has not served to increased trust in the United States or to reduce apprehension regarding the relation between economic penetration via foreign investment and political domination supported by the threat, if not the act, of armed intervention.[8]

In short, it is not difficult to understand why Latin Americans, imbued with the imperialist theory and conditioned by a long series of unpleasant experiences with Europe and the United States, should be generally suspicious of imperialist designs and antagonistic toward United States private investment.

Economic Argumentation. What are the objections to reliance on direct private foreign investment as a development policy based on economic argumentation (as distinct from anti-imperialist ideology)? To begin with, there are a number of arguments that might be classified under the general heading of "offsets to the supposed gains for recipient countries." The net transfer of real resources accompanying foreign investment is felt to be substantially less than the increase in equity claims of foreign investors because so-called foreign investment is usually financed, at least in part, by re-invested earnings (including capital consumption allowances) and with credits obtained from banks and other lenders in the recipient country. In other words, the recipient countries are concerned that national rather than foreign resources are being employed to support the growth of foreign claims against the recipient countries. In the second place, foreign investment (whether financed from net new investment, reinvested earnings, or local borrowing) to some extent prevents a larger volume of domestic investment because opportunities otherwise open to domestic entrepreneurs are exploited by foreigners. A third point is that the contribution of technology and managerial skill supposedly accompanying private foreign investment is illusory inasmuch as foreign firms attract some of the best national human resources from alternative employment and yet deny to this national elite opportunities to rise to top managerial positions and to develop command of advanced techniques to full capacity. A related charge is that foreign enterprises are often falsely capitalized as a result of excessive charges for patented processes, technical assistance, etc.

A second category of characteristic Latin American objections based on economic analysis can be classified under the general heading "unsatisfactory relationship between costs incurred and benefits realized by recipient country." Examples of arguments in this category are: (1) Foreign investors often realize an unnecessarily high and excessive return on the capital goods, technology, and managerial skills committed to recipient countries (especially when account is taken of domestic financial capital and physical and human resources being utilized, in cases where the technology employed is not particularly difficult to command or not especially relevant to the circumstances of the host country, and when the foreign investor is permitted to exploit a monopolist or semi-monopolist position as purchaser or seller); (2) legitimate interests of recipient countries are often violated by sales and other transactions between parent companies and foreign subsidiaries as well as by agreements and other arrangements restricting the ability of the latter to compete vigorously for export markets in the home country or in third countries; and (3) foreign investors are able to exploit any external financial imbalance of host countries to their advantage, especially when the host country currency is overvalued and when the real cost to the host country of servicing foreign indebtedness becomes progressively greater due to deteriorating terms of trade.

In recent years, as most Latin American countries have felt especially constrained by chronic shortage of foreign exchange, there has developed a tendency to attribute some of the blame for this difficulty to excessive foreign debt service, including especially repatriation of earnings on private foreign investments. Latin Americans have made much of the fact that in some years the total of profits and interest remitted to lending countries has exceeded net capital inflows, giving rise to an apparent reduction in the availability of foreign exchange. This view, of course, conveniently overlooks the foreign exchange earnings derived from exports growing out of foreign-financed productive activities, as well as the foreign exchange savings achieved as a result of foreign-financed production for domestic consumption, and numerous other statistical refinements that might well be introduced into a thorough analysis of the overall net balance of payments effects of foreign investment. Nevertheless, given the sensitivity of Latin Americans to their pressing foreign exchange problems, and given the uncertainties they are confronted with as a result of the high degree of variability in foreign capital inflows and related outflows, certainly the view that the balance of payments consequences of foreign investment are often undesirable increases doubts about the advisability of relying heavily on direct private foreign investment as a development policy. A related point that explains the Latin American preference for external financing in the form of intergovernmental loans is that under this arrangement debt servicing is predictable, has some definite terminal date, and is more easily renegotiated—while foreign equity servicing is not so predictable, continues for an indefinite period, and (so it is believed) usually involves a substantially higher foreign exchange cost.

In addition to the above objections, Latin Americans have been especially critical of reliance on private foreign investment in raw materials production for export, whether by agricultural or mining enterprises. There is, first of all, the widely held view that where exploitation of an irreplaceable natural resource is involved, little or no continuing benefit is realized by the host country in the long run—i.e., after the resource has been depleted and profits from the operation repatriated—and that in fact the country might well be left poorer than before. This conclusion depends, of course, on the profit-sharing or royalty arrangements under which such activities are conducted as well as on the factual question of whether, or to what extent, such ventures produce "carry-over effects" in the rest of the economy (e.g., external economies, profits for domestic suppliers, employment for domestic labor, demonstration effects, etc.). Nevertheless, the characteristic Latin American view is that the division of profits is inequitable and that the beneficial carry-over effects are minimal at best—thwarted by the tendency of foreigners engaged in such activities to effectively isolate themselves in "enclaves" and by the practice of denying nationals opportunities for sharing in ownership and management of raw-material-producing enterprises.[9] Another type of foreign investment also singled out for special criticism is that involving electric power generation, transportation, and telephone and other communications facilities. The special concern here is that fee structures are thought to be excessive and the rate of investment and extension of service insufficient. More generally, foreign investments in public utilities are objected to on the grounds that investors fail to integrate their activities adequately with the host country's development plans and that, in any case, citizens of a country should not be dependent upon foreigners for their supply of vital public services. And, finally, there are a battery of special arguments against heavy reliance on foreign investment in manufacturing enterprises, the most significant of which are: that subsidy schemes (protection, import licenses, tax relief, etc.) devised to foster industrialization are diverted to the benefit of foreigners; that foreign-owned enterprises tend to rely too heavily upon imported components and to be insufficiently motivated to develop domestic sources of supply and export markets; and that, because of access to lower-cost financing and more advanced technology, foreigners have an unfair competitive advantage over domestic entrepreneurs.[10]

The list of objections could be extended, although this seems unnecessary to substantiate the basic point that from the Latin American point of view foreign investors generally command too much and provide too little to leave much in the way of benefit for host countries. The main implications of this point of view are: (1) that heavy reliance on private foreign investment is tolerable as a development policy only as long as the imperatives of the immediate situation (especially limited domestic supply of capital and human resources and inability to command sufficient foreign exchange and access to advanced technology through other means) are such as to permit no feasible alternatives, and (2) that Latin American countries must strive to defend their interests against foreign investors by whatever expedients possible while preparing the way for greater independence from foreign financing and substitution of national for foreign ownership of productive enterprises.

Political Considerations.   One important noneconomic force influencing Latin American attitudes toward private foreign investment is the desire of the newer elites to achieve and demonstrate political independence from the United States. For reasons already explained, it is widely believed that a prerequisite for political independence—especially from the United States—is substantial freedom from economic dependence. Another important force is fear on the part of older, established power groupings of the modernizing impact of foreign investment that supports the shift from traditional productive activities and adds to pressures already at work undermining the authority of these groups. A related point, mentioned before, is the desire on the part of vulnerable national interests to curtail competition from subsidiaries of United States companies—especially those resulting from acquisitions of established national enterprises.

Perhaps more important than any of these factors, however, is resentment of attitudes and motivations commonly expressed in the United States—and regularly reported in the Latin American press—that tend to confirm suspicions of imperialist intent. From the Latin American point of view the following are particularly objectionable: (1) statements attributable to United States businessmen and government officials calling for increased private investment in Latin America as an instrument of anticommunist, antisocialist objectives of United States foreign policy; (2) campaigns by business interests in the United States to undermine foreign aid, public loan programs, and commodity agreements in order to force greater Latin American dependence on private foreign investment; (3) petitions by United States investors for guarantees and assurances of favored treatment both from their own government and the governments of the host countries; (4) involvement on the part of United States investors in the domestic affairs of host countries, especially when consisting of alliances with reactionary and repressive national power groupings or of support for political movements thought to be subservient to United States policies and the interests of foreign investors. Also tending to confirm the worst suspicions of Latin Americans are those actions by United States

investors that suggest pursuit of advantage by means of clever accounting practices, sophisticated legal maneuvers, or corruption of
governmental officials.[11]

THE NEED FOR OBJECTIVE REAPPRAISAL

From the foregoing discussion it is evident that there exists a
wide range of opinion regarding what constitutes an appropriate
role for direct private foreign investment in Latin American economic development. These differences of opinion indicate the need
for a reappraisal of all aspects of the foreign investment question
that lend themselves to objective analysis. This reappraisal must be
based on careful research focused on problems and situations that
relate closely to the concerns of policy-makers. Unless the body of
factual information can be increased and the range of interpretation
diminished, the prospect is for continued mistaken calculations and
provocative behavior that promise to be both costly and dangerous
to all concerned.

At the theoretical level a reexamination is needed of the economic
basis of international long-term capital movements, with particular
attention to the factors governing division of gains between capital-
importing and capital-exporting countries. It is also necessary to
appraise the relative merits of various types of international capital
movements from the viewpoints of both supplying and recipient
countries, with emphasis on the advantages and disadvantages of
direct private foreign investment as compared to other types of
external financing. Theories along these lines could, perhaps, best
be tested by making comparative analyses of recent Latin American
and, say, Canadian and Japanese experiences, as well as by comparisons of the historical records and contemporary circumstances
of selected Latin American countries.

A second major area in which research is needed is statistical analysis directed toward establishment of relationships between private foreign investment and other parameters of the development process. For example, studies are needed of relations between foreign investment and the international trade and payments experiences of individual countries. Information is also needed on the relative importance of private investor claims in the structure of the overall foreign indebtedness of the various Latin American countries, as well as on the cost of private foreign equity capital to recipient countries and the nature and amount of debt service burden resulting from direct private foreign investment. As a third example, it would be useful to investigate in specific detail the role of private foreign investment in facilitating technological progress in individual Latin American countries.

Also on the factual side, but in areas less amenable to rigorous statistical analysis, the sources of hostility toward foreign investment in recipient countries need to be identified and the various types of conflicts arising between foreign investors and national interest groups need to be classified and a number of cases examined. A useful approach might be to study the experiences of a large number of investors in order to determine the difficulties with which they have been confronted and the procedures they have followed in coping with these difficulties. An alternative approach would be to examine policies related to foreign investment followed by host country governments, as well as the policies of the United States and European governments and those of various international lending agencies, with the purpose of uncovering inconsistencies and possible opportunities for mutually advantageous accommodations.

Finally, and on a more speculative plane, it would be desirable to appraise the implications of recent trends and policy initiatives for the future role of direct private foreign investment, to weigh these prospects against the requirements for external financing indicated in development plans of individual Latin American countries, and to consider possible new forms of, and roles for, private foreign investment within the context of the Alliance for Progress. In this latter connection, it would be important to distinguish between possibilities for revising the terms under which established foreign-owned enterprises are to be permitted to operate and those which might be appropriate to new private commitments in the future, and to consider by what means and within what limits host countries might appropriately undertake to alter the regulations governing established foreign ventures.

The foregoing research agenda is not suggested without awareness of the difficulties standing in the way of its fulfillment. A high degree of sensitivity on the part of both Latin American governments and United States and other foreign investors exists towards almost all of the topics requiring investigation, and little headway could be made without the cooperation of both investors and host countries. Furthermore, quite apart from the difficulty of devising techniques for objective analysis of the various unresolved questions, investigators in many instances would be closely limited by the unavailability of relevant data. Nevertheless, given the overriding benefit to all interested parties that could be expected to result from a thorough reappraisal of the various points at issue, perhaps it is not naïve to hope that future discussions of the appropriate role for direct private foreign investment in Latin America, based on a progressively growing body of factual information, will generate more light and less heat than has heretofore been the case.[12]

SOME IMPLICATIONS FOR THE ALLIANCE FOR PROGRESS

The question of what constitutes an appropriate role for private United States investment in Latin America has generated much discussion, but very little of the research needed as a basis for a better understanding of the issues. The Punta del Este Charter calls for a large volume of capital flow from the United States, in the form of both intergovernmental loans and private investment. The problem is to devise policies consistent with this objective. The task has been complicated by United States balance of payments deficits as well as by the fact that many Latin American countries have become disillusioned with the Alliance, whether because of difficulty in meeting their own commitments or because of loss of trust in United States motivation and leadership. Nevertheless, in an effort to fulfill its pledge with respect to provision of external financing, the United States government has not only increased the volume of public loans and grants but has also attempted by various means to induce private investors to augment the flow of capital into Latin America. In spite of these efforts, however, the goals established at Punta del Este have not been achieved—largely because potential United States private investors have been reluctant to enter into new and/or expanded Latin American commitments.

This reluctance is attributable to numerous factors—political and financial instability, more attractive opportunities elsewhere, etc.—but in numerous instances the factor of overwhelming importance has been the introduction of additional restrictions on the scope afforded private foreign investment by host country governments. We need not inquire further into the attitudes, motives, and other circumstances underlying these new restrictions, since a rather full range of possibilities has already been suggested. The point we wish to emphasize is that the volume of new private United States investment committed to Latin America so far during the 1960's has fallen far short of the envisaged annual net rate of flow by the drafters of the Punta del Este Charter and, indeed, some Latin American countries have experienced repatriations of profits, interest, royalties, and capital by private foreign investors well in excess of new inflows of private foreign funds.

The fundamental explanation of the shortfall in the private investment flow into Latin America as envisaged at Punta del Este is that potential United States investors have become increasingly wary of the difficulties, risks, and uncertainties associated with new or expanded operations in various of the Latin American countries, while Latin American countries have done little to overcome investor reservations and, in fact, in numerous instances have progressively circumscribed such investment in response to a variety of domestic pressures. If the success of the Alliance for Progress is dependent upon a large and continuing flow of external financing into Latin America, and if a sufficiently large flow is in turn dependent upon a volume of private foreign investment at least as large as that originally envisaged at Punta del Este, the question then becomes that of how to achieve the necessary level of private foreign investment. Several possibilities suggest themselves. Either the United States, acting unilaterally, can undertake to provide additional incentives; or the individual Latin American countries must assume responsibility for the necessary initiatives; or some cooperative schemes might be devised whereby incentives afforded by Latin American countries would be accorded support by the United States such that the decision to encourage private foreign investment, the means to be employed, and the administration of programs would be the host countries' responsibility, while the cost of doing so would be shared by the United States. Let us consider each possibility in turn.

The idea that the United States government should unilaterally encourage direct private investment in Latin America by means of tax inducements, risk insurance, low-cost loans of public funds, free investor services, and so on has been given enthusiastic support by various business and government leaders in recent years. Indeed, not only is there a voluminous record of petitions for government encouragement,[13] but there already exists a substantial number of governmental programs of the sort mentioned.[14] This approach to the problem raises several pertinent questions. First, why should the United States government attempt to push investors into foreign ventures not otherwise deemed sufficiently attractive? Second, what is the most likely outcome of such actions in terms of Latin American reactions and in terms of United States–Latin American relations? And third, what, if any, alternatives exist consistent with United States national objectives and obligations, the interests of the Latin American countries, and the overall spirit of the Alliance for Progress?

The answer to the first of these questions, in the opinion of the writer, is that there is no compelling reason, political or otherwise, for the United States to attempt to induce private investors into commitments in Latin America beyond what the merits of particular projects, as modified by governmental policies and other circumstances in the Latin American countries, appear to warrant in the judgment of prospective investors. On the contrary, there are compelling reasons for the United States carefully to avoid such unilateral initiatives—not only because to do otherwise tends to confirm the worst suspicions on the part of Latin Americans about the motives of the United States, but also because of the danger that counteractions by Latin American countries in efforts to regain the desired degree of control over the volume and type of private foreign investment might lead to further incidents and lingering ill-will which is in the interest of no one—neither the United States, the Latin countries, nor the investors themselves. The answer to the second question, therefore, is that the Latin American countries are inevitably going to be the final arbiters of the terms on which they receive private foreign investment—and quite rightly so—with the result that attempts by the United States to alter these terms by unilateral action is both shortsighted and potentially dangerous.

This brings us to the third question: What are the alternatives? The simplest and most appealing alternative is, as indicated, to insist that any direct encouragement of private United States capital flow into Latin America is the responsibility of host countries. That is, instead of the United States government attempting to push private investors into Latin American ventures, the Latin American countries would be required (not by heavy-handed pressure from the United States, but rather by the urgency of their own circumstances) to decide to what extent they wish to avail themselves of potentially available private foreign capital, and by what means they will attempt to protect themselves from any disadvantages thought to be involved. Not only would this procedure permit the tailoring of the interests of investors to the economic and political realities in host countries, but it would also leave the responsibility for initiative, neogotiation, and control where it properly and inevitably must lie—namely, in the hands of foreign investors and host country governments.

This is not to suggest that the United States government either should or could assume an entirely passive role in the matter. Indeed, under the terms of the Alliance for Progress Charter, as well as under the legislative authority governing United States foreign assistance programs, the government is both morally and legally bound to encourage a larger flow of private investment into Latin American countries—and, again, quite properly so. But the United States is not bound to encourage private investment against the will, or without the cooperation, of the Latin countries themselves; nor, indeed, can it hope to be successful in attempts to do so. Under these circumstances, the proper course for the United States government to follow would be to give appropriate encouragement to the

Latin countries to place greater reliance on the external financing available from private United States investors—but without circumventing the policies of host countries by providing investment incentives in a direct and unilateral manner.

What forms might this encouragement appropriately take? First of all, the United States should carefully avoid reducing, by countervailing regulations or penalties, any incentives offered by Latin American countries. For example, in the case of fiscal incentives Latin American countries are entitled to assurance that the full amount of the intended stimuli will be permitted to accrue to United States investors, instead of being commanded in whole or in part by the United States Treasury.[15] Secondly, the United States government might appropriately assist Latin American countries interested in attracting private United States capital by means of appropriately tailored programs for sharing the costs of promotional programs. For example, agencies of the United States government could provide assistance by serving as information media, or the United States Treasury could offer to underwrite some part of the cost of "technology transfer" to Latin American countries.[16]

The basic questions that arise in connection with these proposals (as distinct from the myriad questions of detail connected with implementation of specific incentive-sparing and cost-sharing arrangements) are two. First, how much pressure, if any, should the United States attempt to put on the Latin countries to offer inducements to private investors and by what means? Second—the perennial dilemma—what actions should the United States take in instances in which additional impediments are placed in the way of private foreign investment by Latin American countries or in which contractual obligations of host countries to United States investors are unilaterally abrogated? These are very ticklish issues on which there doubtless exists a wide range of opinion both within the United States and between the United States and the various

Latin American countries. But these questions should not, and indeed cannot, be avoided. It is better that they be discussed, that some common understanding be established, and that some firm guidelines be developed well in advance of any need to meet a specific situation.

With respect to the first question, in this writer's opinion there is no need for the United States to exert pressure on Latin American countries to offer inducements to private foreign investors beyond the pressure which would automatically result under the schemes proposed. The necessary and appropriate degree of pressure tends to be inherent in the needs of individual Latin American countries for foreign investment. Where the need is greatest, so also will be the pressure to do something about it, and where the need is less pressing, the pressure will be automatically lessened.

The issue bound to arise is, of course, whether public loans and other assistance programs (including the cooperative arrangements here proposed) should be contingent on United States approval of Latin American policies with respect to private foreign investment. It is probably inevitable that there be a substantial gray area surrounding whatever policy is decided upon in this connection, but in this writer's opinion the United States government would be making a mistake if its commitments to provide public loans in support of Alliance for Progress objectives were to be tied too closely to judgments regarding the suitability of Latin American policies toward private foreign investment. On the other hand, the fact is that public funds are not going to be made available for purposes that could easily be financed with private capital—and it is to the advantage of all concerned that this be clearly understood.

There is no simple answer to the second question—what to do when additional limitations are imposed on foreign investors or when foreign investments already committed are subjected to discrimination and harassment. It is worth pointing out, however, that cooperative arrangements of the sort proposed above could be devised in such a manner as to constitute an additional deterrent to such actions by Latin American governments. For example, it might be provided that discriminatory curtailment of incentives to United States investors would result in the automatic cessation of incentive matching and cost sharing by the United States government, thereby making such actions more costly to both the host country and the investor, and causing the ramifications to become quickly and forcibly apparent to all interested parties. Where the terms under which established private ventures are radically revised, or in instances where outright nationalization occurs, it clearly is in the interests of all concerned that some mutually agreeable compensation arrangement be made. The best advance preparation for these situations may well be the insurance and guaranty schemes currently in operation (although there are a number of difficulties with this approach)[17] and also, perhaps, further efforts to devise an acceptable international convention for the settlement of investment disputes.[18]

But the point to be stressed is that an expanded flow of United States private investment into Latin America requires pulling, not pushing. It requires attractive and voluntarily extended invitations from host countries, not unsolicited, unilateral initiatives on behalf of private foreign investors that force host countries to choose between unwilling submission and costly, potentially dangerous resistance.

Notes and References

This study was completed in December 1966 and does not cover developments since that date.

1. Elsewhere I have explained the points and issues discussed in the foregoing paragraphs in greater detail. See my article "Specialization or Diversification? A Basic Policy Decision Confronting Economically Underdeveloped Countries," *The Rice Pamphlet*, XLV, No. 4 (January 1959), pp. 4–18.

2. I have elsewhere attempted to explain the differences between these two types of financial policies, as well as the differences in the underlying rationales. See my article, "Nexos entre la estabilidad monetaria y el desarrollo económico en América Latina: un escrito doctrinal y de política," *Trimestre económico,* October–December 1962, pp. 587–98.

3. This review of the difficulties of, and prospects for, the import substitution strategy of development is based on the following unpublished papers: John H. Power, "Import Substitution as a Development Strategy"; and David Felix, "Beyond Import Substitution: A Latin American Dilemma."

4. A more rigorous and comprehensive presentation of the traditional theory, and references to the basic literature, is to be found in Paul B. Simpson, "Foreign Investment and the National Economic Advantage," in Raymond F. Mikesell, ed., *U.S. Private and Government Investment Abroad,* Eugene: University of Oregon Books, 1962, pp. 503–26. Another excellent review of the theoretical issues, with particular attention to the interests of capital-exporting countries, is to be found in T. Balogh and P. P. Streeten, "Domestic Versus Foreign Investment," *Bulletin of the Oxford University Institute of Statistics,* August 1960, pp. 213–24.

5. For an excellent set of readings revealing representative Latin American attitudes toward private foreign investment (as well as North American attitudes) see Marvin D. Bernstein, ed., *Foreign Investment in Latin America: Cases and Attitudes,* New York: Knopf, 1966. Another excellent source are the essays contained in Raymond Vernon, ed., *How Latin America Views the U.S. Investor,* New York: Praeger, 1966.

6. The best source of the history and specific details of the theory of imperialism is E. M. Winslow, *The Pattern of Imperialism: A Study in the Theories of Power,* New York: Columbia University Press, 1948. For evidence of the influence of anti-imperialist attitudes in Latin America, see Albert O. Hirschman, ed., *Latin-American Issues: Essays and Comments,* New York: The Twentieth Century Fund, 1961, especially Hirschman's essay entitled "Ideologies of Economic Development in Latin America," pp. 3–42.

7. For an enlightening review of the Monroe Doctrine as it has evolved over time see Donald Marquand Dozer, ed., *The Monroe Doctrine: Its Modern Significance,* New York, Knopf, 1965.

8. This brief review of Latin American historical experience with foreigners is based on A. J. Thomas, Jr., "The Evolution of Latin American Attitudes Toward Foreign Investment," in *Conference on Legal Problems of Trade and Investment in Latin America,* Columbia University Law School, New York: Columbia University Press, 1963, pp. 1–20.

9. The additional point that foreign investment in export industries is of

little benefit to developing countries because of a supposed tendency for secular deterioration in the terms on which primary product exports are traded for manufactured goods in world markets is persuasively argued by Hans Singer in "The Distribution of Gains Between Investing and Borrowing Countries," *American Economic Review, Papers and Proceedings*, May 1950, pp. 473–85.

10. The foregoing list of arguments draws heavily on Raymond Vernon, "Foreign-Owned Enterprise in the Developing Countries," in John D. Montgomery and Arthur Smithies, eds., *Public Policy*, Cambridge: Harvard University Press, 1966, pp. 361–80.

11. For a more comprehensive discussion of political factors underlying Latin American attitudes toward U.S. private foreign investment see Miguel S. Wionczek, "A Latin American View," in Raymond Vernon, ed., *How Latin America Views the U.S. Investor, op. cit.*, pp. 3–24. Wionczek's essay also contains some interesting speculation on possible consequences of Latin American regional economic integration for the scope to be afforded private foreign investment in the future (*ibid.*, pp. 24–42).

12. There have been several important recent contributions to an understanding of the role of direct private foreign investment in the development of Latin American countries in addition to those already cited in this paper. See, for example, Leland L. Johnson, *U.S. Private Investment in Latin America: Some Questions of National Policy*, RAND Corporation, July 1964; Victor Urquidi, "Some Implications of Foreign Investment in Latin America," in Claudio Veliz, ed., *Obstacles to Change in Latin America*, London: Oxford University Press, 1965, pp. 91–115; and Peter P. Gabriel, "The Investment in the LDC: Asset with a Fixed Maturity," *Columbia Journal of World Business*, Summer 1966, pp. 109–19. Reference should also be made to Raymond Mikesell's comprehensive study, *U.S. Private and Government Investment Abroad*, cited above, which contains much valuable information and analysis of United States experience. For an extensive bibliography on the subject see Marvin D. Bernstein, ed., *Foreign Investment in Latin America: Cases and Attitudes, op. cit.*, pp. 281–305.

13. Two notable examples are: Commerce Committee for the Alliance for Progress, *Proposals to Improve the Flow of U.S. Private Investment to Latin America*, U.S. Department of Commerce, March 1963; and Advisory Committee on Private Enterprise to Foreign Aid, *Foreign Aid Through Private Initiative*, Agency for International Development, July 1965. See also U.S. Congress Joint Economic Committee, Subcommittee, on Inter-American Economic Relationships, *Private Investment in Latin America: Hearings*, January 14–16, 1964.

14. See, for example, U.S. State Department, Agency for International De-

velopment, *Aids to Business (Overseas Investment)*, September 1965.

15. For a comprehensive description and analysis of various so-called tax-sparing proposals (and of related questions such as tax deferral, tax treaties, western hemisphere trade corporation legislation, etc.) see Peggy Brewer Richman, *Taxation of Foreign Investment Income*, Baltimore: Johns Hopkins Press, 1963, especially pp. 80–88 and 125–29.

16. The latter proposal is similar to recommendations made by the Advisory Committee on Private Enterprise in Foreign Aid, *Foreign Aid Through Private Initiative*, *op. cit.*, pp. 36–45.

17. On this, see Marina von Neumann Whitman, *Government Risk-Sharing in Foreign Investment*, Princeton, Princeton University Press, 1965, especially pp. 69–120 and 304–49; and U.S. Congress Joint Economic Committee, Subcommittee on Inter-American Economic Relationships, *Private Investment in Latin America: Report*, May 1964, pp. 13–18.

18. The International Convention recently submitted by the World Bank to its members for ratification provided for conciliation and arbitration procedures to be employed by foreign investors and contracting states in the settlement of investment disputes. The provisions of this document have been unanimously rejected by all Latin American countries as unacceptable.

RICHARD S. THORN

The Alliance for Progress: The Flickering Flame

T H E Alliance for Progress is a bold attempt to establish a new political and economic relationship between the United States and the nations of the Americas. It is one of the most significant political and social experiments of our time and will have a prominent place in the history of international relations independent of its immediate success. For the United States the Alliance is the most important development in its relations with Latin America since the Monroe Doctrine. Its implications go far beyond the solution of the immediate problems that led to the signing of the Charter of Punta del Este in August 1961—implications that are only now being fully comprehended. The economic and social goals the Alliance sought to achieve in a decade, it is now obvious, cannot be attained in that time, but will require

Richard S. Thorn is Professor of Economics in the University of Pittsburgh.

the labor of generations. Consequently, the success of the first five years of the Alliance can be measured only by the degree of comprehension that the nations of the Americas have acquired of the principles embodied in the Charter, by their understanding of the enormous problems confronting the implementation of the Alliance, and by their willingness to seek solutions to these problems. It still remains to be seen whether the Alliance will provide the basis for a new era of international cooperation between developed and developing nations of the western hemisphere.

The Charter of Punta del Este, which formally established the Alliance for Progress, introduced two new principles into inter-American relations, which give the Charter its distinctive character. It was the first major western political document to link economic and social progress directly within a framework of democratic institutions. In an attempt to establish a new political relationship between the nations of the hemisphere, the countries of the Americas, excluding Cuba, agreed that they would join together *multilaterally* to harness the energy and resources of the region in order to launch a common attack on the economic and social problems of the region. Hemispheric problems of economic and social policy were to be subject to multilateral discussion and, where agreement was reached, multilateral decisions were to be taken. The embodiment of this concept in the Charter modified in some degree the doctrine of nonintervention in the domestic affairs of countries, which had formerly been the basis of inter-American relations.

The Charter was conceived of by its supporters as a revolutionary statement meant to rekindle the spirit of men:

We, the American Republics, hereby proclaim our decision to unite in a common effort to bring our people accelerated economic progress and broader social justice within the framework of personal dignity and political liberty. . . . Today, in ancient lands, men moved to hope by the revolutions of our young nations search for liberty. Now we must give a new meaning to that revolutionary heritage. . . . It is our inescapable task to fulfill these just desires—to demonstrate to the poor and forsaken of our countries, and of all lands, that the creative powers of free men hold the key to their progress and to the progress of future generations.[1]

However, the road between revolutionary proclamations and their realization is a long and difficult one, often marked by violence. The force of ideas is irresistible, but their power, like that of water falling on stone, comes more from their persistence than from their immediate impact. What follows is not a final judgment on the Alliance, but a record of the impact the Alliance has had on the nations of the Americas in the brief period of its existence and an examination of some of the problems it has encountered.

THE CHARTER OF PUNTA DEL ESTE

The Alliance for Progress was engendered by a combination of political and economic forces that threatened Latin America with economic collapse and a resurgence of totalitarianism from both the left and the right. The situation required a radically new approach if democratic institutions in the Americas were to be preserved and strengthened. To appreciate the nature of the Alliance and its problems it is necessary to review briefly the events that led to the signing of the Charter in August 1961.

Stimulated by a brisk demand for its exports, Latin America enjoyed a decade of relative prosperity following World War II. However, at the same time competitive products from alternative sources of supply began to appear on world markets while output continued to grow in Latin America. Eventually, the prices of Latin American exports, buoyed up by postwar shortages, the Korean War, and the Suez Canal affair, collapsed, falling by more than 20 percent between 1955 and 1959. The most enlightened economic policies could not have averted the severe adjustments imposed upon the economies of Latin American countries by the structural changes in world markets. Unfortunately, in many cases the policies pursued aggravated rather than moderated the problem of adjustment.

While this was occurring in the economic sphere, there was continued deterioration in East-West relations, manifested dramatically in the Berlin blockade and, later, in the building of the Berlin wall. This deterioration was accompanied by a step-up in communist activities in Latin America, where economic conditions increased the receptivity of the intellectuals and the masses to political programs promising radical changes in existing conditions. The attack on the Vice-President of the United States by a mob in Venezuela in 1958 and Castro's overthrow of the Batista government in 1959 and his growing ties with Communist nations crystallized opinion in the United States and focused the nation's attention on Latin America.

Meanwhile, in August of 1958, President Juscelino Kubitschek of Brazil urged all the presidents of the governments of the Americas to mobilize the institutional and economic resources of the region in a coordinated attack on common problems of underdevelopment in an "Operation Pan America." This led to a series of meetings of representatives of the countries of South and Central America and the United States, which culminated in the signing of the Act of Bogotá in September 1960.

This Act restated the need to accelerate economic development and to carry out a social welfare program in each country in order to meet the most urgent needs of the Latin American people. It called for agrarian and fiscal reforms, more housing, expanded public health and education programs, and greater external assistance. The United States reluctantly agreed to support the creation of a Latin American common market and to consider stabilization of Latin American export prices, and the Latin American

governments reluctantly agreed to encourage private foreign investment in their countries. To carry out its objectives the Act of
Bogotá created two important instruments: the Inter-American
Development Bank (I.D.B.) with an initial capital of $1 billion
to implement the Act's economic objectives, and the Social Progress
Trust Fund with an initial capital of $500 million (to be admin-
istered by the I.D.B.) to implement the Act's social objectives.

These were the historical antecedents to the Alliance for Progress
proposed by President Kennedy in March 1961. He called for a
bold new solution to the problems of Latin America, asking for an
ideological as well as a material response to Communism that would
go beyond the reforms proposed in the Act of Bogotá. He established a task force under Adolf Berle and Thomas C. Mann to
study the problem, and he solicited views from diverse sources
within the United States. Richard Goodwin, one of the President's
brightest assistants, drafted the new proposal, which added four
elements to the principles of the Act of Bogotá: (1) It recognized
explicitly the necessary complementarity between economic and
social progress. (2) It established specific goals by which progress
towards the objectives of the Alliance could be measured. (3) It
requested countries to draw up long-term development plans to
achieve these goals. (4) It pledged $20 billion of external resources
to implement these plans during the decade of the Alliance.

The principal economic goals established for the Alliance decade
were:

1. A rate of growth of per capita income sufficiently high to
   assure self-sustaining development and to lessen the gap between Latin America and industrial nations. A minimum
   growth in per capita income of 2.5 percent per annum was
   believed necessary to achieve these objectives.
2. A more equitable distribution of income in order to make

the benefits of economic progress available to all economic and social groups.

3. The establishment of more diversified economies, less dependent on a few export commodities.
4. Acceleration of the rate of industrialization.
5. Increased agricultural productivity.
6. Encouragement of programs of agrarian reform.
7. Elimination of adult illiteracy by 1970, and access to a minimum of six years primary education for each child.
8. A minimum increase of life expectancy of five years; provision by 1970 of potable water to not less than 70 percent of the urban and 50 percent of the rural population.
9. Increased construction of low-cost houses for low-income families.
10. Maintenance of price stability.
11. Strengthening of economic integration and intra-Latin American trade.
12. Reduction in the fluctuations of the foreign exchange earnings derived from the export of primary products and the creation of better access of Latin American exports to foreign markets.

To carry out these goals countries were to submit national development plans within eighteen months of the signing of the Charter of Punta del Este. The proposed $20 billion minimum flow of external capital was subsequently broken down by the Secretary of the Treasury as follows: $11 billion from U.S. government sources; $3 billion from U.S. private investment; $3 billion from other foreign investment, largely European; and $3 billion from international financial agencies.

In launching the Alliance, President Kennedy in an address before the Washington diplomatic corps declared, "Our unfulfilled task is to demonstrate . . . that man's unsatisfied aspiration for economic progress and social justice can best be achieved by free men working within the framework of democratic institutions. . . . Let us once again transform the [western hemisphere] into a vast crucible of revolutionary ideas and efforts."[2] The key word in President Kennedy's address was "revolution." He referred to it again and again, linking the Alliance with the American and Mexican revolutions and the Latin American wars of independence. The President set a revolutionary criterion for change, and the call for a "revolution," albeit a peaceful one, was seized upon with great fervor by many people in North and South America. However, many members of the President's audience were not so enthusiastic, and the reception of the President's words by Latin American officials was generally one of skepticism. A notable exception was President Rómulo Betancourt of Venezuela, who embraced the Alliance and pledged his full support.

THE IMPLEMENTATION OF THE ALLIANCE

The agreement of all the governments of the Americas except Cuba to the principles of the Alliance was a major achievement in itself. The next step was to implement these principles, and here two major weaknesses in the Charter became apparent immediately:

1. The Alliance had almost no policy-making or executive-administrative machinery to formulate and implement policy and carry out its objectives. The Committee of Nine, originally set up to evaluate the development plans submitted under the Alliance, made a valiant attempt to become the conscience of the Alliance, but lack of resources and legal authority made it ineffective.

2. The pledge of $20 billion over a decade had been made by the government of the United States, which had authority to commit only its own funds. Europe was not represented at

Punta del Este and treated the Alliance as an American show. Attempts to obtain multilateral support for the Alliance via the Development Assistance Group (D.A.G.) of the Organization for Economic Cooperation and Development (O.E.C.D.) were rebuffed. Private U.S. investment in Latin America continued to decline.

As one Latin American expressed it, "The Alliance was born a cripple forsaken by its parents." Raúl Prebisch, the influential Argentine economist who was appointed coordinator of the Committee of Nine, surveyed the situation of the Alliance after one year and concluded there was little hope for the Alliance's achieving much economic and social progress. He left the Committee of Nine to return to the Economic Commission for Latin America and subsequently went on to organize the United Nations Trade and Development Conference.

Drawing up national development plans represented a substantial effort for most of the Latin countries. Unfortunately, many plans were prepared hastily on the basis of limited data and, consequently, were often technically weak. Even more unfortunate was the fact that none of the plans were adopted as national policy. In fact, the policies of some of the governments were often at wide variance with their development plans.

Widespread suspicion hindered the Alliance from the beginning, not only in Latin America but in the U.S. State Department as well. In Latin America many regarded the Alliance merely as an instrument of U.S. foreign policy. This view gained further credence when the United States made it clear that it wished to negotiate its part of the Alliance bilaterally (a position that was approved by countries as diverse as Bolivia, Chile, and Mexico). The result was that after two years of operation the Alliance for Progress and the Agency for International Development (A.I.D.) were largely synonymous in the minds of the public and of most government officials.

In 1963 Dr. Raúl Saez, who replaced Dr. Prebisch as coordinator of the Committee of Nine, called on the Inter-American Economic and Social Council to reorganize the Alliance and create a multilateral policy-making body. In response to this plea, the Council selected two of the most influential Latin American statesmen, former Presidents Alberto Lleras Camargo of Colombia and Juscelino Kubitschek of Brazil, to suggest changes in the Alliance. They presented separate reports in June 1963 but made similar recommendations.

Both agreed that the lack of "political will" on the part of the Latin American countries and the United States was the biggest obstacle. The lack of will in Latin America was, in the words of the economist Joseph Grunwald, partly due to the concern "whether the Alliance for Progress represents traditional U.S. foreign policies under a new guise and whether it will be used to further U.S. political and economic objectives which might not necessarily be in the best interest of Latin America."[3] The lack of political will on the part of the United States is more difficult to explain since the Alliance came into existence largely as a result of U.S. initiative. Some critics blame this lack of will on the bureaucracy of the State Department and A.I.D.[4] This was only partly true. Another contributing factor was the strong difference of opinion between the State Department and A.I.D., the former being more concerned with political reliability than economic development.[5] The President's advisers in the Alliance, Goodwin and Schlesinger, however, proved to be poor agents to implement the policies of the Alliance, for they lacked firsthand experience of the political and economic realities of Latin America. Partly because of their influence, and partly because of his own predisposition, the President failed to delegate the necessary authority to the agency responsible for carrying out the Alliance.

The absence of a clear chain of command, the presence of multiple lines of communication, and the dispersion of decision-making undermined the influence and authority of the United States and its most effective spokesman for the Alliance, Teodoro Moscoso, the Coordinator of the Alliance for Progress. The multiple lines of authority were played upon by several Latin governments,[6] one of the most publicized examples being the dramatic visit of President Victor Paz Estenssoro of Bolivia to President Kennedy in October 1963. Paz succeeded in overruling both the American ambassador and the chief of the U.S. A.I.D. mission on one of the rare occasions when the State Department and A.I.D. were in agreement; in this case, both agencies agreed that U.S. aid should be withheld until the Bolivian authorities carried out the reforms to which they were committed by the foreign assistance agreement between the two governments. These events did not go unnoticed in Latin America— or in the U.S. Congress. Congress had been led to expect rapid and substantial progress. When this did not occur, it began an unrelenting attack on the Alliance which, continuing to this day, placed A.I.D. permanently on the defensive. Such a position has proved to be inappropriate for an agency charged with fomenting a peaceful "revolution."

In an effort to strengthen the Alliance and give it a Latin identity, both Lleras and Kubitschek recommended in their reports that a multilateral political body be created to establish policy for the Alliance, with a seat far away from the "entanglements" of Washington politics. The organization that was finally created in November 1963 in response to the Latin presidents' suggestion was the Inter-American Committee of the Alliance for Progress (Spanish initials: C.I.A.P.), headquartered in Washington.

C.I.A.P. was given a broad charter, general enough to carry out almost any activity that it wished to conduct. However, the lack of interest on the part of Latin American governments and the United

States in implementing the far-reaching concept of C.I.A.P. formulated by Lleras and Kubitschek and the failure to appoint an influential chairman led C.I.A.P. to largely duplicate the functions of the Committee of Nine—with one important exception: C.I.A.P. provided a much needed forum before which the Latin governments could exchange views with the United States and the international financial organizations, a forum which the Committee of Nine did not formally provide. This interchange of views has tended to become the focal point of the activities of C.I.A.P. Discussions between individual countries and the financing agencies and the United States have done much to improve the coordination of financial assistance and improve communications between Latin America and Washington. C.I.A.P., however, still fell far short of the policy-making body proposed by Lleras and Kubitschek.

Under C.I.A.P. procedures, the international financial agencies, the U.S. government, and C.I.A.P. annually discuss with individual countries how the goals of the Alliance are being met and the progress they are making in implementing national development plans. C.I.A.P. issues recommendations on the basis of these discussions. In some cases, future financial assistance is made conditional on the submission of a letter of intent to the chairman of C.I.A.P., outlining the government's program for the coming year or two. The acceptance of this letter does not automatically guarantee the availability of financing for the country's development program. It does, however, represent general agreement on the part of the financial agencies and the United States as to the general criteria by which the government's overall economic performance will be judged. The country must still bargain bilaterally with each agency for funds.

C.I.A.P.'s annual reviews reduced the Committee of Nine to a technical body without decision-making functions. When the Committee was reduced from nine to five members, the remaining members resigned en masse, in June 1966. As of February 1967, the five members had not been replaced.

The United States' attempt to establish a European link with the Alliance through the Development Assistance Group (D.A.G.) of the O.E.C.D. received a cold reception. The Europeans preferred to deal with individual Latin American countries on a bilateral basis, although Canada, Sweden, and Germany channeled small amounts of tied assistance through the Inter-American Development Bank.[7] In addition, the Bank has been permitted to float several small bond issues in European capital markets.

In short, the Alliance has never been implemented in its two most important institutional aspects: It has not achieved an organizational identity, and it lacks a political body to set policy for the Alliance and an executive body to carry out these policies. The creation of C.I.A.P. only partially fulfilled these functions. As a consequence, the concept of the Alliance as a new form of inter-American economic cooperation has not been fully realized. When asked whether the Alliance for Progress is a success, one is sometimes tempted to paraphrase the answer to a similar question about Christianity: "We don't know; it has never been tried." The heterogenous forces that reached agreement at Punta del Este have ironically also agreed tacitly not to implement the multilateral political aspects of the Charter. Thus, when we speak of the accomplishments of the Alliance, we are by and large speaking about the impact of U.S. foreign assistance on the political, economic, and social development of individual Latin American countries rather than about a multilateral, hemispheric approach to these problems.

THE ACHIEVEMENTS OF THE ALLIANCE

The Alliance for Progress called for revolutionary changes in the political, economic, and social structures of Latin American countries. To expect these to have occurred in the brief span of five years would be unrealistic. A more reasonable approach is to ask, as AID itself has done:

To what extent have the countries of the hemisphere addressed themselves to comprehensive, well-conceived national programs of economic and social development? Has a coordinated effort been made to adjust national investment, fiscal, monetary, agrarian and land reform, health, tax and trade policies to the development goals of the Charter? Is there evidence that Latin American Governments have exercised leadership called for in the Charter and significantly modified their policy priorities and programs to reflect the politically difficult goals and guidelines of the Charter? To what extent has attention been given to strengthening or creating public and private institutions whose revamping is essential to the more rational use of national resources.[8]

The answer to these searching questions is generally negative. However, this does not mean that there has been no progress—some progress has occurred in most countries and in many cases it is promising. Nevertheless, the general dedication of political will that would imply an affirmative answer to these questions—such as would be demonstrated by subordinating other objectives to economic growth and social development—has in general been lacking. In fact, political developments on the whole have been disappointing. There have been no less than eighteen unconstitutional changes in government in the five years of the Alliance. The regimes that came to power were largely right wing and military in character, so that while the establishment of any new communist government has been averted (an implied goal of the Alliance), democratic government and the liberation of the individual remains as distant as ever for many Latin countries. The "revolution" has been less peaceful than President Kennedy anticipated and far less complete. It is becoming increasingly evident that there is little the United States or the Alliance for Progress can do to affect the social revolution taking place in individual countries.

The economic and social developments examined below represent significant progress but fall short of the original expectations held for the Alliance. This is not surprising in view of the lack of political commitment and dedication and the relatively small amount of financial support.

The Flow of External Resources

The Charter of Punta del Este undertook to assure a minimum flow of capital to Latin America of $20 billion in the decade of the Alliance. From the beginning there was confusion over whether this sum referred to the gross flow of capital or to the capital flow net of amortization payments. The distinction between the two concepts meant a difference in excess of $1 billion annually. The position C.I.A.P. took was that the sum should be interpreted as the net inflow of capital, since otherwise the capital flow promised would not represent any increment over the net capital inflow that was occurring in the period before the Alliance. The United States maintained that it was the gross inflow which was meant. The debate halted at this point without any resolution of the question.

The average annual net foreign long-term capital inflow to Latin America was slightly over $1 billion during the first five years of the Alliance compared with an average capital inflow of over $1.3 billion in the five years preceding the Alliance (Table 1). On a gross basis, this capital inflow greatly exceeded the Alliance target of $2 billion per annum; on a net basis it represented a substantial shortfall. The decline in the total flow of capital to Latin America was the result of a sharp decline in private foreign investment, which was only partly offset by increased receipts of capital from governmental and international institutional sources.

The aggregate figures, however, conceal a great deal of the impact of the decline in capital movements on individual countries. In the period 1956–60 Argentina, Brazil, and Mexico received approxi-

TABLE 1

NET CAPITAL FLOWS TO LATIN AMERICA (EXCLUDING CUBA)
AND THE CHANGE IN INTERNATIONAL RESERVES, 1946–66

	(1) Balance of goods and services[a]	(2) Net long-term capital[b]	(3) Official capital (investment and loans)	(4) Private long-term capital	(5) Net Private short-term capital and errors	(6) Net increase (–decrease) in reserves[c]
1946–50 (Aver.)	−213	125	−201	326	−75	−163
1951–55 (Aver.)	−617	637	207	430	−83	−63
1956–60 (Aver.)	−1061	1326[d]	375	951[d]	−317	−52
1961–65 (Aver.)	−584	1019	520	499[e]	−236	199
1960	−718	802	321	481	−149	−65
1961	−943	1066	526	540	−373	−250
1962	−693	621	265	356	−308	−380
1963	−67	809	623	186	−242	500
1964	−691	1376	567	809[f]	−268	417
1965	−526	1225	621	604	10	709
1966[g]	−1066	1397	787	610	−51	280

a. The data for 1960–65 do not agree with *IMF Balance of Payments Yearbook* because reserves represent a more recent revision than the rest of the data. Private transfer payments are included.

b. Equal to sum of columns (3) and (4).

c. Total of columns (1+2+5) including International Monetary Fund reserve position.

d. Direct U.S. investment in petroleum in Venezuela averaged $218 million per annum or a total of $1.092 million for the period, according to L. Johnson, "U.S. Private Investment in Latin America since Castro," *Inter-American Economic Affairs*, Vol. 18, No. 3 (Winter 1964), p. 59.

e. Of which U.S. direct investment averaged $97 million per annum (U.S. Department of Commerce, U.S. Overseas Business Investment and Financial Activity, U.S. Senate, Anti-Trust and Monopoly Hearings on the International Aspects of Anti-Trust, April 26, 1966).

f. Mexico accounted for over $500 million of the total private long-term investment.

g. Preliminary.

SOURCE: 1946–60 U.N., *El Financiamiento Externo de América Latina* (New York, 1964); 1961–66 International Monetary Fund. Annual Reports, various years.

mately one-half of all foreign capital going to Latin America, with Argentina and Brazil accounting for one-third of the total. The decline in the flow of capital was heavily concentrated in a reduction in capital movements to Argentina and Brazil, whose share in total long-term capital receipts fell to one-fifth. If we exclude the two largest countries, the sum of net private investment and foreign aid, in general, improved for the rest of Latin America, with a considerable variation among countries.

At the start of the Alliance, disbursements from official sources were slow in getting started, as might have been expected. This did not prevent considerable criticism of the Alliance by Latin Americans. The net flow of official capital from the United States, other countries, and international financial institutions actually declined to a low of $265 million in 1962, considerably below the annual average of $375 million for the period 1956–60. However, by 1965 the net flow of capital from official sources attained a level of $818 million. In the same year the total net inflow of long-term capital was $1.2 billion, almost the level of the most favorable years of the postwar period. Because of the substantial change in the distribution of the capital, it meant increased capital receipts for most of Latin America, excluding Argentina and Brazil. In 1966 the total net inflow of long capital further rose to $1.4 billion due to an increase in official capital inflows.

It can be said in summary that the Alliance maintained the net flow of long-term capital to Latin America at its relatively high level of the late 1950's of a little over $1 billion, but it has not been able to raise it above that level. If, as C.I.A.P. has assumed, a suitable increase would be equal to a net capital flow of $2 billion a year, and this sum were to be distributed in accordance with the formula suggested by the U.S. Secretary of Treasury at Punta del Este, then the responsibility for the $800 million shortfall in the net long-term capital inflow in 1965 would be almost equally divided among all the sources mentioned by the Secretary—i.e., U.S. Government grants and loans, U.S. private investment, European official and private investment, and international investment institutions. A good part of this shortfall was the result of the lack of investment interest, both private and official, in Argentina and Brazil.

The Alliance was given the task of improving the economic performance of Latin America over that of the late 1950's without having access to any additional foreign resources. This is not to disparage the value of official capital that was received. The availability of foreign resources would have declined absolutely in view of the decline in private investment. It is obvious, however, that under these circumstances any improvements that were to occur had to be achieved largely as the result of greater domestic efforts combined with a certain amount of good fortune, such as an improvement in primary commodity prices. This should be borne in mind in the evaluation that follows.

Economic Achievement

The overall rate of growth of per capita income in Latin America for the period of the Alliance, 1961–65, was only 1.4 percent. These results were heavily weighted by the poor growth experience of Argentina and Brazil, which between them contain half the inhabitants of Latin America. Argentina's rate of growth declined while Brazil's stagnated. In all, only six of the nineteen countries of Latin America achieved the growth target of the Charter of 2.5 percent per capita per annum and, with the exception of Mexico, Peru, and Venezuela, they were all small countries (Table 2).

The rate of growth of per capita product in the first five years of the Alliance, if one eliminates Argentina and Brazil, was an impressive 2.9 percent per capita per annum (approximately 5.5 percent overall). However, the year to year rates of growth are quite

TABLE 2
AVERAGE RATE OF GROWTH OF PER CAPITA GROSS DOMESTIC PRODUCT IN CONSTANT PRICES, 1955–65
(Percentages)

	1950–55	1955–60	1961–65	1961	1962	1963	1964[a]	1965[a]
Latin America	2.4	1.8	1.4	2.3	0.9	-0.8	2.9	2.5
Argentina	1.4	0.9	-0.1	4.1	-5.0	-6.4	6.6	5.6
Bolivia	-1.8[b]	-2.6	2.0	0.9	1.7	2.5	3.3	2.5
Brazil[c]	2.4	2.5	0.2	3.7	1.8	-2.0	-0.5	1.4
Chile	0.9	1.0	1.7	0.9	4.1	0.2	-0.3	2.5
Colombia	2.3	1.1	1.6	2.0	2.1	0.5	1.8	1.6
Ecuador	2.2	1.2	1.4	-0.6	1.3	-0.7	3.2	1.8
Mexico	2.9	2.7	3.4	0.2	1.5	2.9	3.3	2.4
Panama	0.3	2.7	3.9	5.2	6.7	0.8	2.9	2.1
Paraguay	0.3	-0.1	0.5	3.1	-0.9	1.4	0.4	1.8
Peru	2.6	2.0	2.9	6.4	4.6	1.0	2.6	3.4
Uruguay	2.8	-1.1	-1.4	0.6	-3.9	-3.3	0.0	0.0
Venezuela	4.6	2.4	4.2	-3.1	3.9	6.8	3.9	1.8
Costa Rica	3.2	1.5	1.7	-5.0	4.4	2.1	0.0	0.9
El Salvador	2.1	0.9	1.5	4.3	5.7	4.1	4.2	3.6
Guatemala	0.7	2.3	3.9	0.9	-0.4	9.4	2.7	3.9
Honduras	-0.8	1.5	1.6	0.4	2.4	0.3	1.1	2.6
Nicaragua	5.0	-1.3	4.7	2.9	6.7	3.7	4.2	4.0

a. Provisional estimates.

b. 1950/53–1955.

c. A rate of population growth of 3.2 percent per annum was used for the period 1950–60, which is slightly higher than previous estimates.

SOURCE: Pan American Union, *El futura del desarrollo de la América Latina y la Alianza para el Progresso.* Report of the Secretariat to the Fourth Meeting of Inter-American Economic and Social Council (CIES/847), p. 7.

variable and only Bolivia, Guatemala, Mexico, Nicaragua, and Venezuela appear to have shown a steady increase of per capita income. The achievement of self-sustaining growth for most of the countries of Latin America is still not in sight.

The record somewhat improved in 1965. The overall rate of growth for Latin America was 2.5 percent per capita and eight of the nineteen countries achieved this rate of growth or better, with Mexico just narrowly missing the Alliance target. However, such large countries as Brazil, Colombia, and Venezuela failed to achieve the target of the Charter.

The low and high rates of economic growth attained in individual countries were only slightly attributable to the Alliance for Progress. Only three countries—Bolivia, Chile, and Panama—received any substantial amount of aid per capita (Table 3). In these three countries, significantly higher rates of growth were experienced in the period of the Alliance than in earlier periods (cf. Table 2). In the remainder of the countries the amount of aid received was not large enough to play any important quantitative role, although it may have had some qualitative influence. In these countries there is little correlation between foreign aid received and improvements in the rate of growth. For most Latin American countries the major determinants of their economic growth were the domestic policies followed and the performance of their major exports. The upward trend in primary commodity prices was a major factor influencing the general improvement in the rate of growth of Latin America (excluding Brazil and Argentina) which increased from 4 percent in the period 1956–61 to 5.5 percent in the period of the Alliance. The average annual rate of growth of exports increased in the same periods from 0.9 percent to 5.8 percent, respectively (Table 4).

One of the Alliance's important goals was to improve the capability of the countries to mobilize their domestic resources. In order to evaluate these efforts, investment, saving, and public finances

TABLE 3

CLASSIFICATION OF LATIN AMERICAN COUNTRIES ACCORDING TO TOTAL
ASSISTANCE RECEIVED FROM THE U.S. DURING THE
JANUARY 1960 TO MAY 1965 PERIOD

(Absolute and per capita values)

	Absolute Values (millions of dollars)		Per Capita Values (dollars per thousand inhabitants)[a]	
Rank	*Countries*	*Values*	*Countries*	*Values*
1	Brazil	1,316.9	Chile	18,232
2	Chile	734.5	Panama	14,521
3	Mexico	538.5	Bolivia	13,024
4	Colombia	455.5	Costa Rica	9,742
5	Argentina	336.6	Dominican Rep.	7,647
6	Venezuela	303.7	Venezuela	7,417
7	Peru	292.5	Colombia	6,072
8	Bolivia	240.8	Nicaragua	6,009[b]
9	Dominican Rep.	157.2	El Salvador	5,763
10	Ecuador	133.6	Ecuador	5,712
11	Regional	99.2	Peru	5,208
12	Guatemala	88.1	Paraguay	4,800
13	Panama	87.8	Guatemala	4,314
14	Rocap	85.5	Honduras	3,955
15	El Salvador	82.7	Brazil	3,429
16	Costa Rica	66.7	Uruguay	3,389[c]
17	Nicaragua	52.4	Argentina	2,948
18	Paraguay	47.3	Mexico	2,250
19	Uruguay	46.4	Haiti	1,659
20	Honduras	39.8	——	
21	Haiti	37.6	——	
			Median per capita	
	Total	5,243.3	of 1960–64	5,712

a. These figures were obtained by dividing the average aid of the 1960–64
period by the average population of the same period.

b. 1960–64 only.

c. 1960–63 only.

SOURCE: "U.S. Assistance to Latin America," Committee of Nine, Organization of American States (unpublished memorandum).

have been used quantitatively to measure the amount and effectiveness of self-help. Since the statistics used for these measurements are deficient in the Latin countries, the results discussed in the following paragraphs are approximations at best.

TABLE 4

RATE OF GROWTH OF GROSS DOMESTIC PRODUCT AND EXPORTS OF
LATIN AMERICA, 1956–65
(Percentages)

	1950–56	*1956–61*	*1961–65*
All Latin America			
National product	4.7	4.6	4.2
Exports	4.8	0.4	5.8
Latin America, excluding			
Argentina and Brazil			
National product	5.1	4.0	5.5
Exports	8.1	0.9	5.8

SOURCE: *Pan American Union* (CIES/847), p. 10.

Investment. Gross investment has proved to be of limited value as an indicator of performance, as illustrated by the fact that Argentina, Brazil, and Colombia had among the highest ratios of investment to gross domestic product (GDP) and the lowest growth rates, while El Salvador and Nicaragua achieved the highest rates of growth with some of the lowest ratios of investment to GDP in Latin America. The expected relationships between investment and growth appear to lie more in the trend of the investment ratio rather than its absolute amount. This suggests that the type and quality of investment may be as important a determinant of growth as is absolute amount.

Table 5 shows that the trend of gross investment as a percentage of GDP increased in eight of the sixteen countries for which data is available (Bolivia, El Salvador, Guatemala, Honduras, Mexico,

Nicaragua, Panama, and Peru). It declined in five countries (Argentina, Colombia, Chile, Paraguay, and Venezuela) and showed no definite trend in the remaining countries. Changes in the absolute level of investment expenditure over time showed a greater dispersion. The countries of higher per capita income growth (El

TABLE 5

RATIOS OF GROSS CAPITAL FORMATION TO GROSS DOMESTIC PRODUCT

	1960	1961	1962	1963	1964	Average 1961–64	Average Absolute Percent Increase in Capital 1961–64
Argentina	23.9	23.2	23.9	20.6	21.6	22.3	1.6
Bolivia	N.A.	9.9	12.3	21.4	17.6	15.3	4.5
Brazil	14.9	13.7	13.7	13.5	N.A.	13.6	3.8
Colombia	18.3	18.8	18.1	16.4	16.0	17.3	4.5
Costa Rica	17.7	18.1	19.1	18.0	18.9	18.5	4.4
Chile	N.A.a	13.4	12.9	12.5	10.4	12.3	3.7
Ecuador	14.8	15.3	14.7	14.2	14.7	14.7	3.5
El Salvador	N.A.	11.3	10.4	11.1	12.2	11.3	8.0
Guatemala	10.4	10.5	10.5	10.4	12.1	10.9	6.2
Honduras	13.1	11.7	14.4	14.5	14.5	13.8	4.6
Mexico	14.9	14.6	13.8	14.5	16.2	14.8	6.3
Nicaragua	13.4	13.6	14.5	17.0	17.1	15.6	8.1
Panama	16.9	19.0	19.5	20.0	N.A.	19.5	6.8
Paraguay	N.A.	16.9	15.8	15.1	15.7	15.9	3.6
Peru	19.2	20.6	22.5	22.6	23.6	22.3	6.4
Uruguay	15.4	15.4	N.A.	N.A.	N.A.	N.A.	0.0
Venezuela	19.0	22.9	19.9	19.5	20.3	20.3	6.5

a. N.A.—not available.

SOURCE: Pan American Union (CIES/847), p. 158.

Salvador, Guatemala, Mexico, Nicaragua, Panama, and Peru—and the slightly slower growing Venezuela) experienced average increases of 6 percent per annum over the four years 1961–64.

Saving. Gross domestic saving is the part of GDP remaining after all private and public consumption expenditures have been made. Its size is affected by changes in consumption and GDP.[9] One way of interpreting domestic saving is to look at it as the amount of present output set aside to be devoted to the increase of future output. There is, however, only a poor correlation between national saving and the rate of growth of gross domestic product.

The trend in the ratio of saving to GDP increased in Argentina, Brazil, Chile, Costa Rica, Guatemala, Honduras, and Peru from 1962 to 1964 (Table 6). The ratios for the remainder of the countries declined. Part of these results are attributable to the

TABLE 6

GROSS DOMESTIC SAVING AS PERCENTAGE OF GROSS DOMESTIC PRODUCT

	1961	1962	1963	1964
Argentina	18.5	21.1	23.7	23.6
Brazil	15.5	14.7	17.5	18.3
Chile	4.7	8.1	7.2	8.3
Colombia	18.8	16.3	16.9	16.0
Costa Rica	10.4	11.5	10.4	10.8
Ecuador	12.6	13.8	14.3	12.1
El Salvador	11.1	10.2	8.5	8.8
Guatemala	8.5	8.2	10.1	10.2
Honduras	12.2	12.4	12.0	15.2
Mexico	13.4	13.3	13.6	13.3
Nicaragua	12.0	11.3	11.4	N.A.[a]
Panama	11.7	10.4	11.8	N.A.
Peru	21.4	21.7	21.3	24.6
Venezuela	30.5	28.5	28.6	26.4

a. N.A.—not available.
SOURCE: A.I.D., Statistics and Reports Division.

manner in which domestic savings are calculated, the excess of imports over exports being counted as a deduction from domestic savings. As a result, some of the increases in the savings ratios registered were the consequence of a reduction of imports. This in turn reflected a decline in investment (since capital investment in Latin America has a relatively high import content) and adversely affected the rate of growth. Also, reductions in export volume and prices may have stronger effects on saving than a reduction in income from other sources. This is often the case where the export industries are in the hands of higher-income groups, who save a larger part of their income than average-income groups.

The absolute level of savings showed no better correlation with growth performance than the trend shown in Table 5. Absolute savings increased by 25 percent or more in Argentina, Brazil, Chile, Guatemala, Honduras, and Peru in the three years ending in 1964.

Public Finance.   There is only a weak correlation between the growth of public revenue, expenditure, and saving and overall growth; the link is even weaker for qualitative changes in tax and expenditure structures and in administration. The relationship that exists is largely a negative one, for countries that did not achieve a certain degree of fiscal stability generally had a low rate of economic growth. The lack of correlation between self-help measures in the fiscal field and the rate of growth may be in part a question of timing, since these reforms have usually been instituted only after a country has experienced considerable fiscal difficulties, which may have already seriously slowed down the rate of growth.

There is, however, a high correlation between countries experiencing severe fiscal problems and declines in per capita income, as in Argentina and Brazil, or relative stagnation, as in Chile, Colombia, Panama, Costa Rica, and Honduras. Argentina and Brazil ran large fiscal deficits, which were a principal source of the accelerating inflation they experienced until 1965. In Argentina revenues fell both in absolute terms and as a percentage of GDP from

1961 to 1964, after which there was a substantial improvement. Expenditures, particularly capital outlays, declined more slowly than revenues. In Brazil, revenues rose faster than GDP from 1962

TABLE 7

CENTRAL GOVERNMENT EXPENDITURES, REVENUES, AND DEFICITS
AS PERCENTAGE OF GROSS DOMESTIC PRODUCT, 1961–65

	1961	*1962*	*1963*	*1964*	*1965*
Argentina					
Expenditures	17.3	15.5	14.4	14.6	13.7[a]
Revenues	14.2	11.7	10.7	9.9	10.8[a]
Deficit	3.1	3.8	3.7	4.7	2.9[a]
Bolivia					
Expenditures	11.9	13.6	18.8	16.6	15.3[a]
Revenues	6.5	6.8	7.7	8.3	8.1[a]
Deficit	5.4	6.8	11.1	8.3	7.2[a]
Brazil					
Expenditures	18.9	20.1	19.9	22.7	20.0[a]
Revenues	14.4	13.9	14.3	17.0	18.1[a]
Deficit	4.5	6.2	5.6	5.7	1.9[a]
Chile					
Expenditures	20.2	21.8	20.3	20.1	21.1[a]
Revenues	16.9	17.5	16.6	15.6	19.2[a]
Deficit	3.3	4.3	3.7	4.5	1.9[a]
Colombia					
Expenditures	12.3	11.9	10.9	10.2	10.2
Revenues	8.4	7.9	7.3	8.5	8.4
Deficit	3.9	4.0	3.6	1.7	1.8
Costa Rica					
Expenditures	17.3	16.9	17.6	18.7	19.7
Revenues	14.2	14.6	13.3	13.9	14.5
Deficit	3.1	2.8	4.3	4.8	5.2
Dominican Republic					
Expenditures	21.3	22.9	24.1	25.8	—
Revenues	18.1	19.7	22.0	23.7	—
Deficit	3.2	3.2	2.1	2.1	—
Ecuador					
Expenditures	20.4	20.0	19.9	21.1	23.5
Revenues	18.5	18.1	19.8	21.0	22.2
Deficit	1.9	1.9	0.1	0.1	1.3

a. Budget data.

El Salvador					
Expenditures	14.4	12.4	12.9	12.1	13.9
Revenues	12.4	11.5	12.0	11.6	11.6
Deficit	2.0	0.9	0.9	0.5	2.3
Guatemala					
Expenditures	9.4	10.5	8.8	8.9	8.7
Revenues	8.4	8.1	7.5	8.1	7.9
Deficit	1.0	2.4	1.3	0.8	0.8
Honduras					
Expenditures	12.5	12.3	12.4	12.9	12.7
Revenues	10.0	10.4	10.3	10.9	10.7
Deficit	2.5	1.9	2.1	2.0	2.0
Mexico					
Expenditures	8.3	8.6	8.6	8.6	8.3
Revenues	7.6	7.7	8.1	8.0	7.5
Deficit	0.7	0.9	0.5	0.6	0.8
Nicaragua					
Expenditures	10.3	9.3	9.9	10.0	12.7
Revenues	9.4	9.0	9.7	10.6	10.7
Deficit	0.9	0.3	0.2	+0.6[b]	2.0
Panama					
Expenditures	14.9	15.2	15.9	14.3	15.8
Revenues	13.8	13.6	12.7	13.2	13.9
Deficit	1.1	1.6	3.2	1.1	1.9
Paraguay					
Expenditures	9.4	9.9	9.8	9.5	11.6
Revenues	8.6	9.3	8.8	8.8	9.5
Deficit	0.8	0.6	1.0	0.7	2.1
Peru					
Expenditures	18.5	19.9	22.9	23.6	22.6
Revenues	17.2	17.8	20.8	20.2	19.1
Deficit	1.3	2.1	2.1	3.4	3.5
Uruguay					
Expenditures	16.8	19.6	18.7	18.3	20.4
Revenues	16.4	15.2	14.9	15.1	16.8
Deficit	0.4	4.4	3.8	3.2	3.6
Venezuela					
Expenditures	24.5	21.4	21.2	22.3	23.3
Revenues	23.8	22.4	23.0	22.4	21.3
Deficit	0.7	+1.0	+1.8	+0.1	2.0

b. Plus sign indicates a surplus.
SOURCE: A.I.D., Statistics and Reports Division.

to 1964, but they were able only to reduce the country's fiscal deficit slightly because of the rapid rise in public expenditure. In 1965 sweeping revenue reforms were enacted and the budget deficit declined sharply.

In Colombia and Chile, fiscal deficits and accelerating inflation contributed strongly to the stagnation experienced in both of these countries. In 1965 Chile revised its tax structure and undertook major administrative reforms in the collection of taxes, which resulted in a sharp increase in revenues. From 1964 to 1965 the ratio of domestic revenues to GDP rose from 15.6 percent to 19.2 percent. Expenditures also rose very sharply, however, and in early 1966 the deficit again began to rise. In Colombia major improvements in the tax structure enacted in 1960 failed to yield substantially increased revenues. In an effort to reduce the fiscal deficit the government sharply curtailed investment and abandoned much of its development program.

Only five countries for which pertinent data are available (Colombia, Dominican Republic, Guatemala, Honduras, and Ecuador) made progress toward achieving fiscal equilibrium as measured by the ratio of their fiscal deficit to gross domestic product (Table 7). The fiscal position of twelve countries deteriorated and two remain unchanged. The picture may be somewhat better in 1965 if countries which have budgeted relative reduction in their deficits are able to achieve them. Overall, the picture is not a bright one and several of the countries whose fiscal position improved in the last five years are threatened by a renewed growth in their fiscal deficits caused by rapidly rising expenditures.

Overall Evaluation

The definition of what constitutes self-help is fuzzy and reflects our ignorance of the factors that make countries grow. The commonly employed measures of self-help are only loosely related to observed rates of growth. If we keep this caveat in mind, Latin America, on the basis of the inadequate criteria employed above, has made moderate progress in mobilizing its resources for development. The results would be even more impressive if it were not for the poor performance of the two largest countries, Argentina and Brazil. While Brazil showed some signs of improvement in 1966, the Argentinian situation continued to deteriorate.

The validity of the present measures of self-help—investment, saving, and public finance—is becoming more and more doubtful. Recent studies have indicated that what national savings are spent on is as important as their magnitude. While more investment in any particular country generally will produce a higher rate of growth, the difference between success or failure appears to lie in *how much* higher a rate of growth it will produce. This consideration once again throws us back to the seemingly naïve idea that the type of investments made and the efficiency with which they are utilized is important. What is needed is not only more investment but better investments.

The role of government action also must be reexamined. There appears to be no consistent relationship between public saving and public investment or the relative size of the government sector and economic growth. It is reasonable to anticipate, however, that in the long run adequate rates of economic growth in most countries will require some growth of the public sector. For the time being, the only quantitative relationships that seem generally to hold are negative ones. Fiscal disequilibrium seems to be associated with low growth rates, and high rates of government investment seem to be correlated with low levels of private investment.

What appears to be emerging from the myriad official and private reports on the progress of the development efforts of various Latin American countries is that the *political will* to develop is more important than any quantitative criteria of self-help. Countries that have wished to develop and have been willing to subordinate other objectives to attain their goal have achieved it almost irrespective of differences in their particular circumstances. The U.S. Department of Agriculture made a study of twenty-six developing agricultural countries in an effort to determine why some grew successfully and others did not.[10] Twelve of the countries studied showed successful growth. These twelve countries all had different climates, levels of income, educational levels, cultural patterns, government systems, and relative scarcity of land. What they did have in common was a well-defined program of agricultural development and the will to implement it. Few countries in Latin America have displayed a willingness to sacrifice competing political or social goals for economic development.

Although the self-help efforts of the countries have been unimpressive in the first five years as measured by the goals of the Alliance, there is undoubtedly a growing trend for countries to increase their development effort and to give economic growth a higher priority. This has occurred even in countries that experienced unconstitutional changes of government. The commitment to formulating systematic priorities and development goals and to strengthening their institutional capabilities has become stronger. Excellent surveys are available of the economies and diagnoses of the economic problems of most Latin countries. The next step is to translate the substantial knowledge acquired by national planning groups and international agencies into political action, which will require a better integration among the responsible agencies. No country in Latin America has successfully solved this problem.

Social Achievements[11]

One of the major thrusts of the Alliance for Progress was its attempt to make a direct attack on social conditions while simultaneously trying to achieve higher rates of growth. This aspect of the Alliance was meant to appeal to the mass of people in Latin

America and to improve political stability. The problem unfortunately is enormous in terms of the resources required and has been aggravated by the rate of population growth—2.9 percent per annum in the period of the Alliance, the highest of any region in the world. The goals of short-run economic growth were often found to be in conflict with the goals of rapid social progress in health, housing, education, and agrarian reform. In the countries that tried to accelerate their efforts in social reform, the programs created heavy economic burdens and in many cases impeded immediate economic growth.

As a result, there has been a certain deemphasis of the social aspect of the Alliance in recent years in an effort to concentrate on achieving a higher rate of economic growth that will produce the resources required to carry out the urgent reform programs. Although social progress may not automatically result from economic development, it cannot precede it. Economic growth without social progress may be an empty victory for the people of Latin America, but on the other hand social progress gained at the expense of economic growth may court disaster and lead to an undesirable breakdown rather than transformation, both of the economic and social systems.

Housing. Nearly 40 percent of the urban population of Latin America—45 million of a total of 115 million—live in overcrowded conditions with three or more persons to a room. Many of these units have no running water, sewerage, or any of the public services of a modern community. Fifty percent of the rural population live in similar conditions. In spite of the fact that the Social Progress Trust Fund and member countries provided over $500 million for public housing, housing conditions have deteriorated in the period of the Alliance. This situation led the Inter-American Development Bank to conclude that "given the vast scale of the problems involved . . . international aid alone in this field cannot solve the problem. Although such aid is essential for alleviating a situation which might otherwise become disastrous, the effective solution to the problem can only be assured by the region's own economic growth."[12] The warning is that there is a limit to which economic growth can be sacrificed to social progress.

Health. Partial data on life expectancy and infant mortality indicate there has been a continuance of the favorable trend experienced in recent years before the Alliance. Part of this can be ascribed to better water facilities constructed under the Alliance, which, it is estimated, benefited some 45 million inhabitants, one-fifth of the total population of Latin America. Part of this improvement has also been due to migration from rural to urban areas, where better water and health services are available. However, the improvement in health conditions has been partly at the expense of deterioration in housing and other public facilities—as the result of a rapidly increasing population, which places heavier burdens on public services everywhere in Latin America, thus creating other serious problems.

Education. The countries of Latin America have on the whole made a substantial effort in the field of primary and secondary education. Primary enrollment has increased 6 percent a year on the average and secondary school enrollment 11 percent in the period of the Alliance. Both figures are considerably in excess of the rate of population growth. Unfortunately the quantitative growth in educational opportunity has not been accompanied by a comparable improvement in quality. The same social and economic structure impeding economic growth is also responsible for the defects in the national education systems. Structural reforms of these systems have been initiated in many countries but progress has been slow. Children leaving school is one of the main causes of the low educational levels in most countries, and one in which economic forces play an important role. In the economically more advanced countries, it is the principal reason. In eleven countries for which data exists, only 25 percent of the students who enter first grade complete their primary education. School enrollment is only one of the important educational problems confronting Latin American countries. The educational systems are a reflection of economic and social conditions and so far have followed, rather than led, the structural reforms in other parts of the society of which they are a part.

Land Reform.   The Inter-American Committee for Agricultural Development, in a survey of seven countries which represent about 70 percent of the region's population, estimated that 7 million families were in the category of landless laborers, operators of *minifundia* (small plots), or small farmers with highly insecure and precarious forms of land tenure. To benefit one-half of these families in the next decade would require bringing agrarian reform to some 430,000 families a year, assuming there is no diminution or urban migration. Although every Latin American country except Argentina and Uruguay has passed an agrarian reform law (most of them since Punta del Este), current programs and accomplishments in all countries fall far short of these goals.

Income Distribution.   There are no accurate data on income redistribution for the period of the Alliance or, for that matter, for any period. When general conditions necessary for income redistribution are taken into account—such as a satisfactory rate of growth, industrialization, and the introduction of progressive taxation—it appears that there has probably been little improvement in the distribution of income in Latin America.[13] Some of the countries experiencing satisfactory growth rates (Mexico, El Salvador, Guatemala, Nicaragua, Panama, Peru, and Venezuela) may also have had some improvement in the distribution of income, but these countries account for only one-third of the population of Latin America. The tax system has thus far not been an effective instrument of income distribution, and in many countries it remains regressive.

Social expenditures on health, pensions, family allowances, and housing have been more effective in redistributing income but in turn have created fiscal problems in many countries. It is no coincidence that the five countries with the most extensive social security systems, Argentina, Brazil, Chile, Costa Rica, and Uruguay, are confronted with serious fiscal problems and, with the exception of Costa Rica, with rapid inflation.

Overall Evaluation

The general conclusion that emerges from the experiences of the first five years of the Alliance is that social progress must be geared to the economic progress of the country. Stating social goals independently of economic growth, as was done in the Charter, is not a fruitful procedure. In fact, it may have led to some retardation of both social and economic progress as a result of the premature implementation of social programs not founded upon a broad enough economic base. The dilemma which many countries now confront is that to maintain political stability they require a higher level of social progress than they can afford. The Alliance has contributed to the rising expectations of the people of Latin America without providing a substantially larger amount of resources to meet them. Any sharp increase in productive investments must be made largely at the expense of consumption and social expenditures. If Latin America is to achieve a viable development, it must attain a higher rate of growth in national product with which to finance higher levels of productive investment and social expenditure. Social expenditure does not have to be abandoned but the rate of growth must be moderated to a level that can be financed out of the increment in national product. In addition, it is essential that the government secure a significant portion of the increment in national product in order to provide necessary public services and facilities and make the expenditures required for achieving social progress and political stability. A contribution to the solution of this dilemma lies in promoting the idea that economic growth, by offering greater employment and higher wages, is also a social program—provided that part of the increment to national product is used for improving the social conditions of the mass of people.

REFLECTIONS ON THE FIRST FIVE YEARS

What general conclusions may be drawn from this brief survey of the economic and social achievements of the Alliance of Progress in its first five years? The Alliance came into being only because two diverse trends in world affairs happened to coincide: a decline in international commodity prices and the deterioration of East-West relations, which led to a confrontation in the Americas. When juxtaposed, it hardly seems probable that these two events would produce a document like the Charter of Punta del Este. Although the Charter set impossible goals for most countries and provided only modest additional resources to achieve these goals, the fact that it was drawn up at all and that twenty republics of the Americas endorsed its principles is its real achievement. Moreover, a beginning has been made in the social and economic revolution foreseen by the Charter. Planning for economic development is taking root, tax reforms have been enacted, and most countries have passed land reform measures. Even though some of these measures have not been implemented, a first step has been taken, due in part to the Alliance.

The fulfillment of the goals of the Charter are still distant, but sound principles for economic and social progress have been established. This is more important than the progress made in any specific time period. The task ahead is to keep to the guidelines established and to implement the principles of the Charter as rapidly as circumstances will permit. If the intellectual leaders of the Americas can persist in their dedication to the ideas underlying the

Alliance, they will eventually carry their people and politicians along with them. The masses of the Americas are only beginning to awake to the reality of the twentieth century. Not until they comprehend the political, economic, and social ideas that have swept over Europe and the United States since the turn of the century will they become a constructive force in achieving the goals of social and economic progress stated in the Charter. If the Alliance in any form is to be a success, it is necessary now for the intellectual forces in Latin America to mobilize the people. The job of the Alliance is a task for half a century, not half a decade. In retrospect, this period of the Alliance may be looked back upon as a period of consolidation, one in which the original concepts were redefined and solidified into a more realistic basis for a program of action.

THE FUTURE OF THE ALLIANCE

Victor Alba, in his incisive book, *Alliance Without Allies*, in reply to the question of what is needed to get the Alliance back on the road laid out at Punta del Este, paraphrased Danton:

For the Alliance to triumph three things are essential . . . . politics, yet more politics, and always politics. By this I mean that the fundamental prerequisite, from which all others derive, consists of placing the problems of the Alliance on the political level, in conceiving of the Alliance not only as an administrative, technical, economic, or social plan but rather as an essentially political one. . . . The millions of dollars, the experts, the good intentions are not enough. What is needed is a sane, effective well-thought-out political concept.[14]

To instill just such a new political initiative into Inter-American relations, President Johnson has proposed that a meeting of the Presidents be convened. If such a meeting takes place (the preparatory meeting in Buenos Aires of foreign ministers was postponed because of the overthrow of the Argentine government by a military junta), the lessons of the first five years of the Alliance provide ample guidance for its direction.

The Alliance for Progress lacks a political identity apart from U.S. foreign policy. It requires the crystallization in concrete terms of the political concept of multilateral cooperation proclaimed in the Charter. The experience of the past five years indicates an essential need for a politically responsible policy-making body to provide guidance to the Alliance and to make it an alliance in fact as well as in name. The political desire on the part of the United States and Latin American nations to create and support such a policy-making function is more important than the formal location of this function. The Council of the Organization of American States or the Inter-American Economic and Social Council (C.I.E.S.) could assume this function. The directives of such a policy-making body would provide the Inter-American Committee of the Alliance for Progress (C.I.A.P.) with the necessary guidance and support to enable it to become the executive body of the Alliance, charged with implementing the decisions of the Council and reporting to the Council on problems and progress. The new Committee of Experts (which is to replace the Committee of Nine) would then become the technical arm of C.I.A.P.

In the area of substantive issues, C.I.A.P. should broaden its interests so as to include not only the evaluation of the progress of individual countries in achieving the Charter's goals and the financing of country development programs, but it should also enter into areas of concern affecting the welfare of the hemisphere. As long as the discussions of C.I.A.P. center on the financial aid required to implement individual national development programs, they will necessarily be of a bilateral character—between the country concerned and the financial agencies. However, there are issues of hemispheric importance which would benefit from multilateral discussion and action.

For example, C.I.A.P. might take a deeper interest in the trade problems of Latin America and a more active interest in the role of economic integration. Latin American agricultural products have received discriminatory treatment abroad, partly because of the failure of Latin American countries to form an effective political bloc to protect their interests.[15] It has been customary for the British to speak for Commonwealth interests and for France to protect the interests of its former African colonies. It would be reasonable for the United States to insure that Latin American interests were duly taken into account in world councils, and it could do this by consulting multilaterally with the members of C.I.A.P.; it would thus be in a position to promote inter-American policy abroad.

C.I.A.P. could also perform a valuable function in coordinating and improving technical assistance among Latin American countries. This is a particularly promising area for the Alliance since it is an area in which Latin Americans can make substantial contributions.

If the Alliance is to become a success it must become embroiled in "politics and more politics." The past five years of the Alliance have destroyed any illusions that the problems of Latin America are technical problems that can be solved simply by the correct choice of economic strategy or the application of a sufficient amount of foreign resources. Unless we conclude that most Latin American ministers responsible for economic policy were either foolish or irresponsible men who insisted in rejecting patently superior policies when they were available, we must conclude that economic objectives were subordinated to what were thought to be other more important goals.

The Alliance was created as an essentially political concept. It was a brilliant attempt to gain the political support of the people of Latin America and the United States for a program of economic and social development. In the words of President Kennedy, it was meant to be an "ideological answer" to Communism, an inter-American manifesto. As we have seen, the appeal to the governments of the Americas to establish a new type of political coopera-tion has not been answered. Multilateral cooperation has been subordinated to the narrower short-range goals of individual coun-tries. The failure of the Alliance to achieve its political and economic goals need not be discouraging if we recognize why it failed. It is a failure largely because no new political organization has been created. If this is recognized, I have no doubt the time will come in the near future when the countries of the Americas will make an attempt at closer political and economic cooperation, this time with fewer illusions about the magnitude of the problems. Foreign as-sistance, which seemed to loom so large at Punta del Este, is now recognized to play, quantitatively, a marginal role in the economic development of Latin America. It is widely recognized that the great bulk of material resources (financial and human) that are needed to accelerate economic and social development must come from within the region itself.

The United States on its part, I believe, should reappraise its views on "regionalism" and conclude that its assumption of a position of leadership in the western hemisphere is not inconsistent with its role as a world leader. It is difficult to foresee whether the "one world" vision of the late Wendell Wilkie will come about as a result of the successive consolidation of regional groupings, or as a result of their dissolution and the formation of new larger groupings. One can see both of these opposing influences at work today. There is little doubt however that the failure of the nations of the western hemisphere to devise an effective political alliance for the attain-ment of common economic and social goals is impeding the de-velopment of the region, including the United States. The principles of the Charter of Punta del Este provide a valid basis for this alliance and should not be abandoned until they have been given a fair trial. The first five years of the Alliance could be the beginning of the most important political development of this century in the relationship between developed and less developed countries.

POSTSCRIPT

Since the above was written in February 1967 the much delayed meeting of Pan-American Presidents was held in April 1967. The meeting might have been delayed indefinitely had it not been for the perseverance of the United States. The timing of the meeting was not propitious. The preparatory work and agreement necessary to make such a meeting a success was incomplete and it was doubtful until the last minute if all the Presidents would attend. As it turned out only the President of Bolivia was absent. In view of the adverse conditions under which the second meeting at Punta del Este took place, the outcome was more successful than could have been anticipated.

The United States made it clear it could promise little additional economic help to Latin America, and with the exception of one or two sharply dissident voices most countries acccepted this situation without the usual denunciations of U.S. policy. Latin comprehension of the U.S. position was partially due to recognition of the U.S. burden in the Vietnam war. The general attitude was one of sober realism that there is no Santa Claus or magic economic formula to solve the problems of Latin America. This attitude provides a more promising setting than the unrealistic public optimism generated by the first meeting at Punta del Este.

The basic weaknesses of the Alliance, the lack of any politically responsive policy making body and the absence of any executive authority, were not dealt with directly. The conclusion of the meeting was a declaration in which the Presidents stated their intention:

1. To create a common Latin American market beginning in 1970 which will be substantially completed by 1985,
2. Lay a physical foundation for Latin American integration through the initiation of multi-national projects.
3. Increase trade earnings
4. Make efforts to modernize rural living conditions and increase agricultural productivity.
5. Promote education for accelerating economic development
6. Limit military expenditures in proportion to actual demands of national security.

The only really new points in the declaration were the agreement of the United States to the establishment of a Latin American common market and the support of multinational projects. The plea to limit military expenditures is, at the present moment, no more than a pious declaration. It does, however, give the United States an excuse to reduce its military assistance and in particular, the delivery of sophisticated weapons. The Alliance, in spite of its multilateral rhetoric, initiated almost no multi-national projects with the notable exception of those supporting the Central American common market.

The creation of a common market has far-reaching implications since it will require the type of multilateral political cooperation that was absent from the Alliance until now. Whether the forces which prevented more effective political cooperation earlier will continue to prevail remains to be seen. Unless new institutional arrangements are created, the prognosis is unfavorable. However, the door is open to the creation of a new institution, now that the United States has withdrawn its formal opposition to the idea of a common market. The creation of a common market organization offers an opportunity to give life to the principles proclaimed in the Charter of Punta del Este.

The next step would be for the Latin American countries to form a common market commission to remove trade barriers in the region and align the trade policies of the Latin American countries in dealing with other regions. Such a commission should be composed of all countries of Latin America, but the day to day operations should be under the supervision of an executive committee composed of Argentina, Brazil, Mexico, the United States, and three other members representing the remaining countries. The executive committee would operate by majority vote, but any decision could be referred to the full council where the principle of unanimity would be applied. The commission should view its task broadly in terms of removing all intra-regional restrictions to trade, and promoting regional development including multi-national projects. The commission would also make a rational division of responsibility between the Economic Commission for Latin America and the O.A.S. whose activities in part duplicate one another at present. One possible division of responsibility would be to have E.C.L.A. concentrate on national planning and international trade while the O.A.S. devoted its efforts to social and sectorial development. The commission would form industrial committees to promote the orderly exploitation of the regions' resources.

While the goal of the commission would be the creation of a common market, it would be recognized that this is a distant objective which can only be achieved slowly after a broad base of political agreement has been reached in many fields and some of the extreme economic disparities have been reduced.

The commission should be based somewhere in Latin America and the economic Secretariat of the O.A.S. should be placed at its disposal.

Most important of all is the United States' position towards such an arrangement. The United States should be prepared to participate fully, both giving and receiving trade concessions. Its aid effort, however, should be kept outside the organization and negotiated bilaterally as at present. The C.I.A.P. would remain in Washington acting as intermediary between Latin American countries, the United States, and financial agencies, in the financing of national development. The experience of the first five years of the Alliance has demonstrated the necessity of the separating U.S. aid effort in Latin America from the Alliance. The political realities in the United States require that its aid program be conducted on a bilateral basis. The attempt to merge U.S. aid with a regional development effort have failed because of the largely unilateral character of the decisions taken with respect to U.S. economic aid. Rather than jeopardize the formation of a true political alliance dedicated to achieving regional development, it is best to accept the reality of the U.S. domestic political situation. Any economic assistance rendered to the Latin American common market should be in support of the programs of the Market.

All countries would contribute to the financing of the common market according to a formula based on population and per capita income.

The success of such a common market depends on its ability to deal with important *practical* questions and to obtain concrete results. This in turn depends on the earnestness of the Latin American countries' support of the common market. A common market, properly organized and not too ambitious in its immediate goals, offers the institutional and political vehicle to create a true alliance for progress.

Notes and References

1. Preamble to the Charter of Punta del Este.
2. President Kennedy's address to the Diplomatic Corps, March 13, 1961.
3. Joseph Grunwald, "The Alliance for Progress," *Proceedings, American Academy of Political Science*, May 1964, pp. 386–401.
4. Cf. Arthur Schlesinger, *A Thousand Days*, New York: 1965, p. 760.

The passage is as revealing a comment about the attitude of the Kennedy palace guard toward the State Department as it is about the attitude of the State Department toward Latin American problems. It is difficult to understand how Kennedy's advisers could be so optimistic about the future of the Alliance and have so low an opinion of the men charged with implementing the United States' part in it.

5. For the full flavor of this, see the posthumous memoir of De Lesseps Morrison (U.S. Ambassador to the O.A.S., 1961–63), *Latin American Mission*, New York: 1965, passim.

6. Again, Ambassador Morrison provides ample documentation and expresses the frustration of U.S. officials who had to operate in this environment.

7. The regular capital of the bank may only be utilized for expenditures in member countries.

8. U.S. State Department, Agency for International Development, "Mid-Decade Evaluation—Alliance for Progress," Washington, D.C.: 1965, mimeo.

9. In most Latin American national accounts the savings data are computed as residuals, and therefore include all the errors and omissions of the other accounts.

10. U.S. Department of Agriculture, *Agriculture in 26 Developing Nations, 1948 to 1963*, Foreign Agricultural Economic Report No. 27, Washington, D.C.: 1965.

11. The data available to measure social progress in Latin America are fragmentary and are often published a long time after they have been collected. Therefore the statements in this section should be regarded as tentative. A survey of recent social progress in Latin America by the U.N. Economic Commission for Latin America will be found in its *Economic Survey of Latin America, 1964*, New York: U.N., 1966, pp. 47–51.

12. Social Progress Trust Fund, *Fifth Annual Report*, Washington, D.C.: Inter-American Development Bank, 1966, p. 74.

13. *Economic Survey of Latin America, 1964*, pp. 48–49.

14. Victor Alba, *Alliance Without Allies*, New York: 1965, p. 189.

15. See Felipe Herrera (President of the Inter-American Development Bank), "Disunity as an Obstacle to Change," in Claudio Veliz, ed., *Obstacle to Change in Latin America*, London: 1965, pp. 230–52.

GERMAN ARCINIEGAS

Intellectuals in the Politics of Latin America

I
T is in the oldest Latin American
tradition for intellectuals to intervene in politics in a form so active
that it surprises observers from the United States. Poets, novelists,
essayists—even grammarians and philologists—have served not
only in congresses, ministries, and governments, but even in the
presidencies of the republics. The liberator of Cuba was not a
general like George Washington, but a poet, José Martí. Even before this, in the Ten Years' War (1868–78), the first that took place
in Cuba for freedom from Spanish domination, it was a musician,
Perucho Figueredo, author of the national anthem of the republic,
La Bayamesa, who organized troops to take the city of Bayamo.

Since the time of Aristotle, politics has been an intellectual exer-

Germán Arciniegas is the former editor of *Cuadernos* and is currently the
Colombian Ambassador to Venezuela.

cise, and assaults by the military, when they try with the sword to resolve problems that require reason, may even be considered a barbarian invasion of this province of the spirit. Of necessity a politician must be an intellectual and use his intelligence to provide a philosophy for his party and his programs. However, one should not deduce from this that an intellectual must be a politician. The poet and the philosopher may be floating in the clouds when it comes to matters of state. It is merely that conditions peculiar to Latin American development have made it more urgent for intellectuals to enter the political arena than conditions in other areas and countries.

What is singular in Latin America is not the phenomenon of the participation of intellectuals in public life, but the extent of their participation. The tradition of intellectuals influencing or participating in government is not lacking in the United States. Woodrow Wilson left Princeton for the White House. Franklin D. Roosevelt, as John F. Kennedy was to do later, placed men, such as the poet Archibald MacLeish, in important government positions; and it was Roosevelt who invited a painter from Brazil, Cândido Portinari, to decorate one of the rooms of the Library of Congress. Perhaps one of the first gestures of Kennedy to make him so welcome a figure in the eyes of Latin Americans was his inviting the poet Robert Frost to his inauguration and having him recite that poem difficult to forget, which says, among other things:

> Summoning artists to participate
> In the august occasions of the state
> Seems something artists ought to celebrate.

The spirit behind these gestures of Roosevelt and Kennedy is one which Latin Americans respond to personally and one which can help strengthen the ties between the northern and southern hemispheres of America. It is significant that under these two national leaders a suitable climate was established for the Good Neighbor policy and for the Alliance for Progress.

* * *

The reason Latin America has had to use the services of intellectuals is bound up with its history and its political nature. The colonies, separated from Spain, proclaimed themselves republics, but in contrast to the English colonies they were inexperienced in the exercise of self-government. The Spanish monarchy was ruled with intransigent and absolute centralism. Spain sent her colonies all their functionaries, from the viceroy on down, and executed all legislation, including the details of the most elementary decrees. To reverse this tradition, to initiate the peoples in the methods of a representative regime, was truly a revolution, similar in part to the revolutions that took place in Europe when monarchies fell. To make the case of Spanish America more complicated and difficult, religion was joined to the state; church and state were like the two heads of the Austrian eagle. In the colonies of North America, the church, or the churches, were one of the initial ingredients of the liberation. From Puritans to Huguenots, they came to the North in search of a free land where they could practice their religion, free from the tutelage of the official church. In Spanish America, religious conflict occurred simultaneously with political independence. The priests who headed the Mexican emancipation were judged by the Inquisition and shot as schismatics; and Juárez, in bringing the movement for independence to an end, gave its laws and its movement a protestant name: the Reform. One understands at once what this signified in a country dominated by the Catholic hierarchy for more than three centuries.

These circumstances of the colonial empire resulted in the case for independence being made in the universities. The generations of essayists, journalists, economists, mathematicians, doctors, students of the natural sciences, and to a lesser degree (although it may seem strange) of lawyers that began to rebel within the ancient colonial universities from 1780 on, formed the first of the groups with revolutionary spirit that continued to appear for the next 190 years. It is not out of place to remember today that the wars of independence in the Spanish colonies were accomplished by placing students at the front of the armies, and that those who headed the squads of mounted insurgents became generals through popular acclamation and not through promotion in the professional ranks. Perhaps the only notable exception was General San Martín, an army man trained in Europe.

In the United States agitation within universities is now developing in the Latin American style. For the first time, the desire of the intellectual element to modify certain trends in the affairs of state and to make its presence count in the great debates of the nation is manifesting itself. Generally, the political careers of United States senators, ambassadors, Secretaries of State, and governors are not necessarily connected with the academic or intellectual life of the country. In the nineteenth century, no one would have expected the author of *Uncle Tom's Cabin*—a novel that influenced the nation's history—to be proposed as a candidate for the presidency; or that in this century any of the more famous novelists would be thought of for the same office. Because there is no tradition in the United States of artists and intellectuals being selected for political leadership, people ask themselves how it was possible that in Venezuela, the first freely elected president, was a writer who had been a novelist, and nothing more than a novelist.

This man, Rómulo Gallegos, had captured in his novels—*Doña Bárbara, Reinaldo Solar, Cantaclaro, El pobre negro*—the problems of the fields, of the city, of the workers and farmers; he painted the anxiety and suffering of the Venezuelan people at a time when it was not possible to present these publicly in a direct way. Dictatorships like those of Juan Vicente Gómez in Venezuela, Machado or Batista in Cuba, Leguía, Sánchez Cerro, or Odría in Peru indicated to sensitive men that the best avenue of political expression was the novel. Nothing has so effectively influenced the formation of a new consciousness of the problems of the land in Peru or Ecuador as the novels of Ciro Alegría or Jorge Icaza. Even today, years after the publication of his *El mundo es ancho y ajeno*, Alegría is trying in the Peruvian Parliament to convert into laws the themes of his seemingly fictional work. The Latin American novel has been a humanized form of polemics often considered peculiar to essays or political speeches; but in dramatizing social issues in novelistic invention a writer adds to the essential truth of a problem an element of passion and combat more effective than all academic or political literature.

When democracy was introduced for the first time in Venezuela, Rómulo Gallegos was the best point of reference that the Venezuelans had for creating an image of a new political life, for the only connecting link between the ordinary Venezuelan and politics was a collection of novels. The same thing occurred in Santo Domingo, when the stories of Juan Bosch carried him into the presidency. Dictatorships not only demolish the physical and moral foundations of democracy, but they impede the formation of political cadres qualified for administration. To choose a novelist as the head of government might be a crazy adventure. It implies placing an excess of confidence in a man who works with the imagination and the typewriter. It may happen, and I believe that it has happened in the two cases mentioned, that such a man will not be able to adjust his capacities to the necessities of the moment, with the result that he will turn out to be an incompetent administrator.

Dictatorships may be the cause for the lack of qualified administrators, but there is also an external responsibility for the reasons that Latin Americans, moving between hope and desperation, rush headlong down the illusory path of choosing their artists to guide their new democracies. This responsibility belongs to those who have lent their support to the dictatorships, and who have provided them with arms and credits. Paradoxically, for one reason or another, the dictators who ruined Latin America enjoyed an international economic base of good prices in foreign markets which no government of democratic reconstruction has had since.

Gallegos did not have the political ability of Rómulo Betancourt to evade the Venezuelan tempest nor the insight of Raúl Leoni. It is doubtful that he could have survived the emergencies that faced Betancourt's government, or that he could have administered the country and at the same time coped with an undeclared war waged first by Trujillo and later by Castro. Betancourt lived the novel that Gallegos was unable to invent, escaping the personal attack that was prepared for him with excessive cunning from Santo Domingo, and fighting against guerrillas supplied with all the instruments that the strongest Communist power in the hemisphere could place at their disposal. But it cannot be forgotten that the novels of Gallegos were one of the stimuli that gave strength to the Venezuelan people to rid themselves of oppressing despotism.

In the history of postrevolutionary Mexico, José Vasconcelos as Secretary of Public Education imparted decisive new directions to the recovered nation. He was the great inspiration of his time. He arranged for the walls of schools and palaces to be filled with revolutionary colors and saw to it that Rivera and Orozco had walls on which to paint. He multiplied the libraries, stimulated the education of the Indians, transformed the university and gave it its famous motto: "The spirit will speak through my race." He was a man of letters par excellence. In his most brilliant period, he alternated admirable speeches on Madero and messages of prodigious vitality directed to the youth of America, with studies on Indian philosophy or a tentative metaphysic for the use of the Latin Americans. However, if he had won the presidential election, it is difficult to imagine that he would have guided the country with the firmness and security of the less intellectual politicians who later succeeded to power. Lázaro Cárdenas complemented the work of Vasconcelos. The hard hand of the general brought to fruit the mystical imagination of the thinker.

There is the case of a very Latin poet who became the best administrator of an island, as they well know in the United States—the poet Luis Muñoz Marín, governor of Puerto Rico. In all of Latin America there have been numerous examples of poet-governors, and their success has been varied. Even the pure poet, the most poetic of poets, by reason of his very power of imagination, may be very useful and capable of providing extraordinary departures in public administration. There is, more recently, the example of Jaime Torres Bodet. I think even more informed people in the United States are not aware of the many sides of Torres Bodet and don't know him as ambassador, as the transitory but very effective director of UNESCO, or as the hard-working Secretary of Public Education of Mexico. He has been a great inspiring force of administrative efforts that transcend ordinary limitations. The literacy campaign alone that caused Mexico to raise the budget for public education and health to levels much higher than the figures for the army is an example for the rest of America and for the world. His original system for establishing prefabricated schools, which leave the factory in trucks and spring up like miraculous mushrooms in the most distant provinces, gave education a mobility that is now being tried in other continents. But it should not be forgotten that Torres Bodet was a great poet before he was a public official. It can almost be said that there is a very human contradiction, pleasing to thoughtful men but yet surprising, between this patient builder working in public administration and the author of the poem that begins:

Thou singest so that no one may hear the footsteps
Of the impatient guest
That comes and goes, in thy soul, night and day.

The success of Torres Bodet in the Secretariat of Public Education in Mexico has caused the lawyer president who now governs the republic to name a novelist, Agustin Yañez, to succeed him.

In approaching the human reality that surrounds him, the Latin American intellectual inclines to revolutionary formulas. This tendency is explained by the urgent need to find a fundamental change, which, according to José de Castro, must take the form of a war against hunger. This attitude on the part of the intellectual is not new. The agrarian problem has been expounded in Buenos Aires since the time of Rivadavia, and the solutions offered then were extremely radical. In reconstructing the Argentine Republic, revolutionary writers and poets—Sarmiento, Mitre, Alberdi, and Echeverría—organized the country in a spirit contrary to that of the Spanish crown and of the despotism that had been reestablished by Rosas. The America we know today, comes from a series of dictatorships like that of Rosas. In Argentina itself there was the devastating dictatorship of Perón, who, while he had his philosophers, ran into the streets crying "Workers yes, books no!" in the style of the Spanish general who declaimed a similar absurdity from the rostrum of Maestro Unamuno in Salamanca: "Down with *la inteligencia!*" In Peru there was a succession of dictators from Lequía to Sánchez Cerro and Odría. Odría, in reestablishing his dictatorship, invaded the cloisters of San Marcos with the tanks acquired by Peru during the Second World War. In Colombia there were twelve years of suspension of constitutional order that ended with the dictatorship of Rojas Pinilla. During that period, the Colombians had to publish their books abroad, and censors burned the volumes they tried to bring into the country. With Pérez Jiménez, Venezuela, the birthplace of Simón Bolívar, closed the barbarous cycle that had prevailed for a large part of its history. Even though Juan Vicente Gómez had, in the author of *Cesarismo democrático*, one intellectual who would defend him, the Venezuelan university generation that was formed in exile in Colombia, in Chile, and in Argentina acquired sufficient strength to rescue the nation from Gómez's dictatorship. It is not necessary to recall what happened in the Caribbean area. It is an embarrassment of which no one is ignorant.

*   *   *

How may Latin America's troubles today be summarized? The Marxist babblers have picked up the phrase "structural change" and are applying it with rigor as an easy answer to any situation. But in spite of its excessive use, which tends to make the phrase commonplace, the words have significant meaning for the problems of Latin America. In reality, Latin America lacks the solid economic base necessary for survival in the international arena. It has seen the prices of what it produces slide down to the bottom of the abyss; it has seen itself converted into an island surrounded by common markets to which it has offered its products, only to be paid at charity rates. There is no country that does not have to face this desperate situation. Colombia lost more than $100 million a year because of the drop in the price of coffee; with this deficit as a point of departure, there is no political stability possible. Ecuador is facing ruin, because Japan, instead of buying bananas from Ecuador as formerly is now buying them from Formosa. Europe and the United States have made an effort to stimulate the revival of Asia and Africa but have ignored Latin America. In another part of the world, an empire of coffee, cacao, bananas, and copper is growing; in Latin America a gloomy economic vacuum is developing, and no one seems able to suggest a means of filling it. We have a damaged economic structure in the southern part of the hemisphere. We are countries of moderate development, unexpectedly deteriorating. Facing this situation, which demands a comprehensive review, intellectuals are searching for radical solutions. In the meantime, they are receiving stimuli from abroad, which explains the expansion of Marxism in the universities. The seriousness of this situation lies in the simplification of the Marxist formulas provided by contending powers. The truth is that Latin America's problems are too complex for simple Marxist solutions.

Latin America has had more revolutions than is generally realized. Today we have not one revolution but many, each with its own character and orientation. We have tried many solutions, and it cannot be said that those originating from intellectual sources have been the least felicitous. The really unhappy ones have been those which came from the military. I have heard that many people in France, in Germany, and in the United States prescribe a heavy hand to keep us in order. We have already endured this, and it has always brought us into catastrophic situations. Heavy-handed regimes have ruined nations like Argentina (which was decisive in aiding European nations when they were hungry), or have brought forth governments of unlimited corruption, whose beneficiaries still travel through France, who maintain palaces with twelve liveried servants, and whose horses compete in the Derby.

At this moment, three types of revolutions can be distinguished in Latin America—those taking place in Mexico, Cuba, and Chile —the study of which will be useful for observing the extent to which the intervention of intellectuals is beneficial or catastrophic. In all of these cases, the fact must be accepted that the intellectual —through the newspapers, from the classrooms, by means of verses and novels—has been the operative instrument in the formation of a revolutionary mentality.

The Mexican revolution was not only fought by guerrillas such as Zapata and Pancho Villa, the latter accompanied by men like José Vasconcelos and Martín Luis Guzmán, one a philosopher, the other a novelist, but in its beginnings was led by Francisco Madero, a lawyer. In institutionalizing itself, that is to say in converting itself into a legal reality, Mexico's revolution passed from the barracks to the university; its leadership passed from presidents who were generals to presidents who were lawyers. Among the revolutions of our time, the Mexican is the one that offers the most positive results. The Chilean revolution was engendered by a group of scholars, who were the foundation of the Christian Democratic Party. Its point of departure was a basic study of the Chilean reality in seminars of academic investigation and in books. Those scholars who came to power did so by rising above the traditional parties of the Right and Left, offering more radical solutions than either. The Cuban revolution is dominated by criteria as much Marxist as militarist. Its original objectives have been diverted, until today the revolution is consecrated to establishing bases of guerrilla military training that serve movements (in Cuba called movements of liberation) destined for Africa and Asia, as well as for Latin America. In a certain sense it is an anti-intellectual revolution, and perhaps for this reason attracts many intellectuals outside the island.

Of these three revolutions, that of Mexico was accomplished without any aid whatsoever from any foreign country. Initially directed against North American and English capital with petroleum interests, it has succeeded in raising the country to an economic and social level that makes Mexico today the least dependent country of Latin America. Chile began its revolution under most unfavorable conditions. It is a country whose economic bases have been hard hit, and whatever can be done in cooperation with the

Alliance will barely perpetuate the early achievements of the revolution. All in all, it is a very Chilean revolution, which has managed to sustain popular confidence in pure electoral competition without executions. The course of the Cuban revolution is obscure. It is not possible to obtain information freely—information like that from Mexico, Chile, or even Russia—in order to formulate a precise judgment. There have been suspicious occurrences, such as the disappearance of "Che" Guevara, or significant ones, such as the army purges and previous purges in the diplomatic service and government cadres. One wonders how Russia will be able to maintain her bridgehead in Cuba if there is an internal split. Russia is aiding the revolutionary government to the tune of $1.3 million daily, but the Russian alliance has already resulted in the exodus of some 700,000 Cubans, a political emigration unprecedented in the world, even in America. The exiled Argentinians of the Rosas era and the Venezuelans of the period of Juan Vicente Gómez cannot compete in numbers with these.

It is paradoxical, in studying these three types of revolutions, that the revolution that corresponds most closely to the type of strong government that at times is recommended to Latin America by the partisans of an armed democracy is the Cuban.

* * *

In the Latin American universities today, there exist side by side all the shadings of the left, from the Christian Democrat to the pure Marxist of the old school and the *guajiro* Marxism of the Cubans. Cuba, as the channel of the international movement, invested enormous sums of money in Venezuela, sums that were later reinforced by contributions from Communist organizations in Italy and other countries, with the intention of preventing Betancourt from completing his administration and, later, of preventing Leoni from reaching the presidency. The University of Caracas was the general headquarters of the movement. Although all this cost the Venezuelans millions of dollars because of arson and the destruction of factories and means of communication, the country rose above the situation. In the same way, Carlos Lleras Restrepo, who recently miraculously escaped with his life when the Communists precipitated an uprising in a university and tried to assassinate him, now occupies the presidency of the Republic of Colombia and enjoys enormous prestige. Among the many flags that the opposition unfurled against Frei in Chile was that of Pablo Neruda, a poet of international prestige. But Frei won the day.

As has always been the case, the intellectuals of Latin America are fighting in opposing camps. Without them, the solutions arrived at would be more crude, primitive, and inoperative. With a Latin America in crisis, not only for internal reasons but because of the treatment it receives from abroad, the intelligentsia is indispensable as an instrument for arriving at rational solutions. The more that the world tends to favor the groups in this region that try to substitute force for reason, the darker will be the immediate future of democracy, not only in this hemisphere but throughout the world. Today this continent weighs more heavily in the balance than it did during the first half of the century; and it will continue to weigh more heavily with the passage of the years.

If Communism has enjoyed any prestige in Latin America, it is attributable to its writers and painters: Neruda, Alejo Carpentier, Lombardo Toledano, Diego Rivera—and the many people who have been attracted to them. But until today, the democratic intellectuals have been able to exercise a greater control over public opinion, and if they had a more solid foundation, an economy less unstable than that which the world has reserved for Latin America, perhaps the great bulwark of democracy today would be in that part of the world.

Basically, the Latin American writer will always be politically significant. Undoubtedly Jorge Luis Borges is the most justly appreciated one in Europe and the United States. He emerged as the leader of the literary vanguard in Argentina and enjoys unparalleled prestige in Latin America today. Viewed from without, the work of Borges has nothing to do with politics. His poetry, his novels, and his essays are developed on aesthetic planes. But in that struggle which occurred in his day between a free Argentina and Perón, Borges was the symbol of free Argentina and the man through whom Perón tried to bring freedom to its knees. Like Borges, Alfonso Reyes some years ago received support throughout Latin America for the Nobel prize as a kind of moral endorsement. Reyes, during the most active years of his life, represented the Mexican revolution in both hemispheres as an illustrious ambassador. Russia has appreciated better than anyone the significance of the Latin American writer in political life, and for this reason has organized its formidable machinery in an effort to secure the Nobel prize first for Pablo Neruda, then for Miguel Angel Asturias, and in a less aggressive fashion to satisfy Cuban aspirations for Alejo Carpentier.

The work of the newest novelists—Vargas Llosa of Peru, García Márquez and Mejía Vallejo of Colombia, Rulfo, Carlos Fuentes, and Agustín Yáñez of Mexico—is saturated with social content. If the Cuban revolution, which in the beginning won the unanimous applause of Latin American writers, had maintained itself within a purely American plan, it would not have lost so many well-wishers in so short a time.

John F. Kennedy was able to melt a large area of resistance to the United States by promoting the Alliance for Progress, but more with his attitude than with the Alliance itself. Since his death, the Alliance has been forced to cope with the natural difficulties implicit in such a plan. Latin Americans think that these difficulties can be resolved only by a spirit akin to Kennedy's, a spirit which they do not find in his successor. The invasion of the Dominican Republic, in bypassing the charter of the Organization of American States has, in this sense, been ill-fated. Each hope has eventually brought frustration. But it is evident that if a formula like Kennedy's were revitalized and inspired by a spirit as enthusiastic and radical as his, it could set forth in bold relief the conditions and qualities of a workable system, as Communism has done in Cuba.

Like the university professor or the politician, the writer is seeking a solution, or at least the hope of a solution—not moved by enthusiasm in search of new ideals, as in other epochs, but under the stifling pressure of an overpowering urgency. The greatest difference that exists between men of today and those of yesterday is that today we live under the threat of imminent collapse, a collapse that could mean an unprecedented catastrophe for the entire hemisphere, and we are not sure how to prevent it.

J A M E S   M A L L O Y

Revolution and Development in Bolivia

B O L I V I A illustrates dramatically the interrelated dynamics of political revolution and development— particularly economic development. The party that made the Bolivian revolution of 1952 something more than a traditional *golpe de estado*—the Movimiento Nacionalista Revolucionario (MNR) —viewed itself as a movement of national liberation and national development. The MNR justified its violent seizure of government and its major overhaul of Bolivian society as the only means capable of achieving economic development in a country that a parasitic oligarchy had kept locked in a state of backwardness. Despite the lasting marks of its *revolución nacional*, the MNR never did achieve its chief goal of creating a modern developed nation state in Bolivia. This paper will examine the MNR's rise to power and its ultimate failure in terms of the more general problems of the pursuit of development through revolution in underdeveloped regions.

The Bolivian revolution is not an isolated phenomenon. The

James Malloy is Assistant Professor of Political Science in the University of Pittsburgh.

goal of the rapid economic development of national state units has become a generalized political motive, hastening the formation of a variety of political organizations and behaviors in all regions of the world. Most of the convulsions which we call revolutions have been justified, at least in part, by the avowed goal of rapid economic development. Bolivia is undoubtedly part of a more general political-economic process, the specific revolutionary variant of which can be legitimately termed "modern revolution."

The era of modern revolution, most agree, begins with the first great revolution in France in 1789. Modern revolution is distinguished by two basic characteristics. The first was pointed out most clearly by Hannah Arendt in her *On Revolution* (New York: Viking, 1963)—namely, the entrance for the first time into the political realm of large masses of human beings who not only were never previously a prime political factor but whose most basic reality is the day-to-day struggle for sheer physical survival. With these masses the social question (as opposed to the political) becomes a major public issue, and demands born of the necessities of the masses' life situation become one of the critical inputs of political decision-making.

It was also at the historical juncture of the French revolution that the notion of progress took hold, both as an article of faith and a goal for political action. In the last part of the nineteenth century, however, the fomentation of economic development of nation state units became a systematic state policy in leading Western countries. With Stalin and the notion of socialism, in one country, rapid, state-sponsored economic development for purposes of state power appears as an avowed goal in the underdeveloped context. At this point Marxism shifts from an international political ideology to a model of national state-sponsored development in individual countries. Whatever its historical roots, it seems undeniable that rapid economic development is one of the chief goals of emergent elites, particularly in the so-called underdeveloped world.

These two factors—the mobilization of necessity-driven masses, and the use of the state by the elite to hasten economic development—are defining characteristics of modern revolution; they also limit the area within which modern revolutionary behavior is played out.

A third limiting factor is the underdeveloped context itself. Here the question is resources in the broadest sense of the word. In Bolivia, for example, where natural resources are relatively abundant, there is a debilitating lack of capital, technology, and trained and organized human resources. Given the avowed goal of elites— in this case revolutionary elites—the environment severely limits possible behaviors.

After a successful insurrection, such as that in Bolivia in 1952, revolutionary movements invariably split into rival elite factions, struggling not only over power but more fundamentally over how to reorder, redefine, and reorganize society. It is the resolution of the latter type of question that makes a revolution a revolution and not simply a *golpe de estado*. The three limiting factors outlined above set the stage upon which the contending revolutionary elites must act out the *post-insurrection* drama. In the modern underdeveloped context, the normative goal of rapid economic development is so pervasive that even many elites with minimal previous commitment to this goal are forced to proclaim it publicly as a primary goal. The post-insurrection problem of reordering and reconstructing at some point becomes a battle over alternative courses and institutionalized orders related to this goal. In a real sense, the post-insurrection battle eventually boils down to alternative political models for the goal of rapid economic development.

There are a number of points of contradiction and hence conflict in the modern revolutionary situation as defined here. The first involves the potential clash between a mobilized mass demanding immediate alleviation of need and the development goal of elites, which requires accumulation and investment. In the underdeveloped context especially, an investable surplus demands deferral of consumption (i.e., the denial of the mass demand). The situation is even more complex: Given the resource situation, often the only immediately available resource is sheer human energy, mobilized, organized, and directed toward the development goal; but such additional mobilization will undoubtedly spur an increase in demands for gratification, and so the circle goes endlessly on.

The conflict between investment and consumption is common in all underdeveloped situations, revolutionary or not. In the revolutionary setting it is exacerbated by the need to build support for a new political order and specific governments to run it. All political systems face the problem of balancing demands and supports. The task is hard enough when there exists a functioning system, but obviously it is extraordinarily difficult where one is trying to bring a new system into being just after the former system has been destroyed.

In very general terms, there are three ways support can be generated for a political system: (1) mobilization of commitment, that is, affective identification; (2) force; (3) satisfaction of demands. The first is the ideal but, given that a revolutionary situation is by definition one in which affective commitment to various orders is, to say the least, in question, it is rather problematic. Within the revolutionary movement there may be fervor, especially in the early days, but since the movement is usually based on mobilization by means of slogans and ideologies expressing previously frustrated demands for gratification, the fervor is usually based on anticipation of gratification soon after an insurrection has succeeded. Supportive behavior, if not identification, could be achieved by force, but this raises moral questions for some types of projected orders; it is unstable and uneconomical over the long run and presupposes that contending elites have the wherewithal to use force, which is not always the case. Thus, we are left with satisfaction of demands and are right back to the clash between consumption and investment, but in an even more serious context.

In recent years there have been a number of important examinations of political models of economic and social development. Common to these efforts is the view that particular development regimes and the orders they create represent alliances or combinations of important social groups, which provide a basis of power for imposing a "development solution" on a society. The notion of a political model employed here follows the Weberian tradition of the use of ideal typical constructs. The fashioning of specific concrete models is viewed as the result of the resolution, through conflict in specific situations, of two fundamental problems: (1) control and (2) social costs.

The problem of control involves the issue of which contending elites—identified with which social segments of a society—will play the major role in redefining and reordering the society after it has been "revolutionized." The second problem is directly related to the first and raises the question of which group or groups shall carry the greatest burdens in the process of economic development. That some groups bear more of the burden of the unit's gross advance seems historically undeniable and unfortunately unavoidable. These two problems are critical and their presence feeds the already gestating violence of conflict in the modern revolutionary situation. The resolution of the problems of segmentally based elite control and the allocation of social costs is the stuff of which the contemporary revolutionary dilemma is made.

PREREVOLUTIONARY PATTERN OF DEVELOPMENT

Bolivia, while surely a "backward" country, does not suffer so much from underdevelopment as from the persisting effects of a relatively recent twentieth century pattern of "misdevelopment."

To understand the national revolution of 1952 and the difficulties which have beset Bolivia ever since, one must first grasp, at least briefly, the pattern of real development and modernization that Bolivia experienced in the first quarter of this century. The pattern can be defined as one of skewed and eventually truncated development. The revolution of 1952 was in part a reaction to this pattern; the inability to reorganize the country since 1952, either politically or economically, is due in large part to the persistence of certain situations created by the previous development pattern.

The basic factors of Bolivia's twentieth century economic growth have been dealt with quite adequately in a number of recent works.[1] As is well known, the important factor was the phenomenal growth of the tin industry in Bolivia between the 1890's and the early 1920's. Less well known is the concomitant establishment after 1898 of a "liberal" political order in Bolivia. With tin came economic modernization in the form of infrastructure development, machines, techniques, and (in the 1920's) large corporate concentrations. Three corporations, Aramayo, Patiño, and Hochschild came to control over 80 percent of tin production. With the civil war of 1898 came political modernization in the form of the politics of interest groups, political parties, and ideologies. Moreover, the new liberal governments consciously pursued development through policies designed to promote the growth of tin.[2]

Despite periodic falling off in demand for tin, production and profits rose steadily into the 1920's. But tin was about the only product to benefit. In the civil war of 1898, the locus of power in Bolivia had shifted from southern Bolivia and an elite based on silver and land to northwestern Bolivia and an elite based on tin, bureaucracy, and land. The "new" Bolivia, associated with the cities of La Paz, Oruro, and Cochabamba, grew, while the rest of the country slipped backward. Thus Bolivia became increasingly reliant on tin for its existence.

A major result of this development pattern was an economic bifurcation of the country. Denied anything but the most meager impulses, agriculture languished and in most of the country became a subsistence affair. The modern child of the Spanish *encomienda*, the *hacienda*, remained the basic organizing unit of rural Bolivia, guaranteeing thereby the atomization of the countryside and the dominance there of traditional social, political, and economic interests and values. There evolved, in effect, two separated socioeconomic systems: a national semimodern system, centered in La Paz and based on tin, and a local semitraditional system, dispersed throughout the rural countryside and based on the *hacienda*.

Thus, in the latter part of the nineteenth century and the first two decades of the twentieth, Bolivia experienced relatively rapid economic development. The development was not a generalizing internal process, but rather a limited, externally linked process which led to a skewed developmental pattern, overreliance on a single, extractive industry, and the tying of the local economy to external factors outside local control.

The dangers of this situation became apparent after 1925. Declining tin prices taxed the ability of the local industry to bring home the former high returns. More significantly, however, the quality of the ore mined began to drop; the lifeblood of the industry was in irretrievable decline. Another trend of negative significance was the narrowing gap between imports and exports reflecting a flow, not of capital goods, but of food and manufactured goods; Bolivia was learning to live off the outside. The negative drift first manifested itself in the country's financial structure. Unable to meet its debts and maintain large budget outlays, the government stumbled through a number of increasingly severe financial crises.

In 1929 the bottom fell out. The government went bankrupt, and in 1930 Bolivia defaulted on its external debt. Amidst financial crises, the country embarked on a major foreign war with Paraguay (the Chaco War), which was financed by internal borrowing and the printing press. The resulting economic disaster was more severe in the tin industry itself. In 1929 the industry reached its peak output, never again to be attained. From 1929 to the present, the pattern of tin was reversed (continual decline, punctuated by brief recoveries but within a permanent downward trend). Key structural features of the drop were declining qualities of ore and rising production costs. The industry shifted steadily to a labor-intensive effort, and labor costs became a larger and larger input. Concomitantly, there began a process tantamount to decapitalization, evidenced by the fact that the estimated value in 1952 of the plants of the big three companies was only $1 million more than the estimate for 1929.[3]

THE STRUCTURE OF THE OLD ORDER

The economic factors discussed above obviously had important sociopolitical consequences. The original development impulse occasioned important shifts in the structure of power and social stratification. The old ruling class was pushed aside but not destroyed. A new power elite arose, particularly in La Paz. The new elite, however, was not an entrepreneurial class. It was made up of high-level professionals—especially lawyers—who in one way or another worked for the big tin interests. Unlike the previous conservative oligarchy of the South, the tin interests did not directly exercise political power. They were content to let the new elite exercise power directly, while they functioned as an interest group pressuring government for favorable policies. As tin was the only dynamic economic base, the companies were, in effect, the only real interest group of note. Given their economic position and the current ideological values of the new liberal elite, it is not surprising that the companies had a significant hand in shaping state policy. Indeed, it would not be an exaggeration to say that, in matters of concern to them, they controlled the state.

As a result of the mono-economic motor and its obvious slowing down in the 1920's, mobility channels began to harden. Having no independent economic base, the new elite sought to consolidate its position by acquiring landed status and monopolizing its hold on political power. The upshot was that the new elite adopted the status values of the older aristocratic elite. Before long, the new blended with the old and a new composite national class was forged. There were real differences of value and interest in this upper class, not the least of which were regional. Yet as their later behavior would show, they formed a relatively coherent, self-conscious grouping. As the national system became more static, traditional stratification values became stronger, and the upper class closed off into a small caste-like elite based on race and pedigree as well as wealth. Given its connections in both the tin and land systems, this class of less than 5 percent of the total population dominated the political system and constituted, in effect, the only national class (that is, bridging both systems) in Bolivia.

As the country was bifurcated economically, so was it socially, and, in a sense, politically. The great mass (60 to 70 percent) of the population were Indian peasants who, in the main, were peons on *haciendas*. Aside from a very thin stratum of *mestizo* shopkeepers, craftsmen, and *hacienda* administrators, there was no rural middle stratum to speak of. Thus, the rural system was really a two-class or more accurately a two-estate system with the *patrones* on top and the Indian *peones* on the bottom. The Indian mass lived not as a horizontally self-conscious class but fragmented, in self-enclosed *hacienda* structures. Politically, the peon was ruled not by the national state but by the direct will of his *patrón* or a resident administrator. Clearly the bulk of the country's population did not live in or experience the dynamics of the national sociopolitical system.

The dominant national system was much smaller, but its sociopolitical structure was more complex and approximated the modern tri-class model. Beneath the upper class was a small urban middle stratum (no more than 10 percent of the total population). This middle grouping had a number of important characteristics: (1) it was not a national class, since it lived encapsulated in the tin-based system, particularly in the cities of La Paz, Oruro, and Cochabamba; (2) occupationally, it was connected with the service sector and hence was an economically dependent grouping; (3) it had little self-identity and tended to imitate the style and values of the upper class. Like other such middle groupings, the Bolivian middle group was unadventuresome economically; it valued economic security and assured status.

The upper class (national bourgeoisie) and the middle class (petite bourgeoisie) dominated the national political system between them. The national bourgeoisie provided the high level officials, politicians, and statesmen, while lower-level bureaucrats, etc., were recruited from the middle class. The political system was a case of what Germani and Silvert have labeled the stage of representative democracy with limited participation.[4] Voting requirements effectively excluded all lower class elements, not to mention the peasant mass, leaving the state in the hands of the upper and middle groups (less than 15 percent of the population). The upper class made the essential decisions—with the companies exerting pressure—while the middle class functioned as the political audience and source of democratic legitimacy. The commitment of the middle class to the system was therefore critical.

Beneath the middle group were three additional groupings, only one of which approximated a modern class. The first was a stratum of artisans, craftsmen, and small shopkeepers. Under the import policy of the liberal period, this group was in decline. The second was a group which, with sufferance, might be called a working class. This group was of very recent origin, springing out of the limited development brought on by tin. The first to appear as a self-conscious group were the railway workers, followed later by the mine workers, and finally in the late 1930's and 1940's by a group of factory workers. This working class consisted of perhaps less than 100,000 persons. Moreover, it was not a horizontally cohesive class. The miners lived in isolated camps, and the railway workers were spread along the railnet. The factory workers, the last to appear, were an urban group, over 70 percent of whom lived in La Paz. Aside from these groupings, there were myriad small service-category groups and a heterogeneous subemployed grouping, categorized simply as the popular class (*clase popular*).

PRESSURES FOR CHANGE

It should be stressed that Bolivia, up until 1920, experienced definite economic growth. After 1925, however, growth ceased, and the system became progressively immobilized and stagnant. This declining system was hit in 1929 and 1932 with the cumulated impact of a massive depression and a major war that shattered the Bolivian economy—blows from which it has yet to recover. After 1936, except for a brief spurt in manufacturing and the increased tin demand of World War II, the country experienced chronic economic crises, in which unemployment, inflation, and food shortages have been permanent factors.[5]

Between 1920 and 1930, tensions, set off by increasing immobilism, were reflected with increasing intensity in the political system. At the elite level the process analyzed by Kling[6] became apparent. That is, the elite class was growing by natural processes but its economic base was not; therefore the elite was, in effect, outgrowing its economic base. Simultaneously, increasing pressure was being put on the economic base and status security of the dependent middle group. The artisan stratum likewise was being progressively impoverished by its inability to compete with foreign imports. Finally, the members of the working class, in contrast to their previous existence as urban floaters or peasants, were experiencing aspirations that were being translated into economic and political demands.

At the elite level, there developed a growing struggle over the horizontal circulation of wealth and power which led to the factionalization of political parties, to governmental instability, and to the use of violence. The result was disunity in the elite class and a weakening of the political center's ability to direct the country. Out of this developed an anomalous situation. In response to growing demands from below, the elite showed a definite unwillingness to make structural changes, but its ability to resist such demands as a cohesive power group was eroding internally. Similarly (assuming that the elite, or parts of it, would have wished to direct adaptive changes) elite disarray, governmental instability, and economic stagnation were rendering the elite progressively more incapable of sponsoring such changes. Thus a key prerequisite of revolution was being forged: a status quo elite, unwilling and/or unable to direct adaptation within the existing framework.

Pressure on the middle group manifested itself first in the oncoming generation of youth who, in normal circumstances, would have been destined for upper and middle elite positions. Trained to aspire to political, professional, and bureaucratic positions, this generation faced a stagnating system with fewer and fewer elite career outlets. In the late 1920's this generational blockage set off a widespread university and young professional political movement, in which basic questions about the legitimacy of the entire system, particularly liberal economic ideas, were raised. Within the movement, two rough countersystem tendencies appeared: a nationalist reformist tendency, and a revolutionary socialist tendency. Out of this dynamic, was shaped the second key ingredient of a revolutionary situation—the formation of counter-elites.[7]

Finally, pressure on the middle stratum itself, which was to become most severe in the postwar inflation, began to shake the loyalty of this grouping, so critical for overall stability. Pressure on the artisan stratum drove it toward the incipient working class groups, creating by the 1920's a combined artisan-labor movement. The clash of this movement from below against the static system and increasing pressure by the elite pushed the movement in a consistently radical direction. Thus, among these diverse groupings reacting to different problems, the final ingredient of a potential revolution was created—mobilizable counter-publics.[8]

OPENING OF THE REVOLUTIONARY SITUATION

The depression and the Chaco War intensified these tensions, bringing them to a head in 1936 and bringing Bolivia to a revolutionary situation. Between 1936 and 1952 a process of challenge and response began, characterized by violence and incipient civil war. Between 1936 and 1939 the country was ruled by two reform juntas backed by young nationalist reformers.[9] Between 1939 and 1943 a fused status quo elite held sway and attempted to reverse the process. In 1943 a second young nationalist military alliance seized power; in 1946 the alliance was toppled, and a reunited status quo elite again ruled. By 1952 the ruling elite had fallen apart internally. Finally, after a brief period under a status quo military junta (1951–52), the famous revolution of April 1952 took place.

Throughout this period, economic deterioration and inflation proceeded apace. Reformist counter-elites, unable to hold onto power once they had seized it, or to initiate lasting reforms, became progressively more radical and revolutionary. Inflation, violence, and general instability deepened the alienation of the urban middle stratum. A seesaw process, in which labor demands were met by reform governments only to be violently negated by reaction governments, politicized the labor movement into a cohesive revolutionary force. This was particularly true of the miners, led after 1944 by the Federación Sindical de Trabajadores Mineros de Bolivia (FSTMB), which, carrying the memories of army-smashed strikes in 1942, 1947, and 1949, became an intransigent revolutionary vanguard.

Of the many counter-political organizations that sprang up after 1936, the most important for our purposes was the Movimiento Nacionalista Revolucionario (MNR). The MNR is traceable to the nationalist reformist tendency manifested among young professionals in the late 1920's. Ideologically, it was a diffused grouping, which projected its goals in a vague concept of national renovation. Between 1936 and 1939, although not yet a party, the grouping grew and expressed its theoretical viewpoints in a new daily, *La Calle*, and in practice through participation in the military reform governments of Davíd Toro and Germán Busch. During this period the ideology was defined as state socialism. In theory and practice the doctrine was statist and envisioned reforms imposed from above by a small elite. It envisaged state control over the economy, particularly tin, and a corporate state structure to be founded on compulsory unionization, under state control, of all economically productive strata. It did not attack private property but sought to guarantee that property would be used in a "socially productive manner." Through a variety of welfare codes, the state would (1) guarantee an acceptable level of living for all groups, (2) arbitrate social disputes, and (3) coordinate private economic activity to the benefit of national development and autonomy.

In 1939 the first post-Chaco reform phase was brought to an end by the death of the young military reformer, Germán Busch. Reacting to the threat posed by the post-Chaco effervescence, the status quo interests and parties drew together in a united front dubbed *la concordancia.* Under the presidency of Enrique Peña-randa, a good deal of the reformist thrust was reversed. The most publicized act of the government was the smashing of a mine strike with government troops in 1942, an event that became known as the massacre of Catavi.

FORMATION OF THE
MOVIMIENTO NACIONALISTA REVOLUCIONARIO

Ousted from power by the death of Germán Busch, the young nationalist reformers began to look for means of staging a come-back. In 1941 pre-Chaco nationalists, buttressed by younger post-Chaco figures, formed the MNR. In its early days, the MNR was less a party than a parliamentary and electoral cabal. Playing upon middle-class dissatisfaction, this small group of young leaders— drawn exclusively from déclassé upper-class or middle-class ele-ments—placed a sizable body of representatives in the national congress. Using the congress as a forum, the MNR harassed the government and criticized the existing Bolivian political economy.

In speeches and documents, the MNR developed a doctrine heavily laced with Marxist analysis, emphasizing the concepts of nation, state, and economic development. Its basic tenet was that, while achieving political independence in 1825, Bolivia had remained an economic appendage first of Britain and then of the United States. The reason was the adoption of a liberal, capitalist state model which allowed foreign financial penetration and the growth of local monopolistic economic interests in the tin industry. These monopoly interests (Patiño, Aramayo, and Hochschild) formed a state within a state and in reality governed Bolivia. They governed by means of an upper class of politicians and landowners which, for all intents and purposes, they owned. Together, the tin companies and this upper class formed a ruling class which the MNR called *la rosca* (the screw).

The orientation of *la rosca* was international and hence antinational. It was this class that had based the local economy solely on tin, thus splitting the country into a stagnant semifeudal agrarian system and a mono-based national system, totally dependent on factors outside local control. Their economic policies allowed the wealth of Bolivia to be exploited to the benefit of other countries and to the steady impoverishment of Bolivia itself. The complete bankruptcy of the policies of this antinational ruling class became unmistakable in the Chaco War when Bolivia was ignominiously defeated by little Paraguay.

The problem of Bolivia was not the typical class exploitation of the Marxists. In Bolivia the nation itself was exploited by a local branch of international capitalism, *la rosca*. The battle was one of nation vs. antination. Socially, the nation was made up of three groups: the impoverished middle class, the working class, and the peasants. Only a movement combining all of these elements —which in reality had a common set of interests—could liberate the nation. Given the backwardness of both the working class and the peasants, the movement would have to be led by the progressive elements of the middle class.

The aim of the movement would be to liberate Bolivia economically and create a truly independent and self-defining nation.

This would be accomplished by state regulation of the economy which would (1) regulate the tin industry, particularly in matters of foreign exchange; (2) sponsor economic diversification and agricultural development; (3) assert state control over public utilities; (4) guarantee protection, dignity, and a decent standard of living to all Bolivians; (5) protect small and medium enterprises, and (6) guarantee Bolivian jobs for Bolivians.[10]

It should be noted that in none of its early programs did the MNR advocate nationalization of the tin industry, abolition of private property, or agrarian reform. It advocated small and medium capitalist operations and the control of, but not abolition of, monopoly formations. It promised to the workers a welfare state and to the peasants little that was concrete.[11] Of some interest was the failure of the party to speak out on suffrage. Thus, while it offered to the masses some extension of social rights, the MNR did not offer a similar amplification of political rights. On balance, the position was reformist; it advocated imposition of reform from above by a state controlled by a middle-class elite; it spoke mainly to the frustrations of the Bolivian middle class of lower professionals and "little men." These elitist and corporatist features, plus heavy doses of anticapitalism, anti-imperialism, anti-Semitism, and anti-Masonry, caused the MNR to be branded as fascist.

In those early days, the tri-class nature of the MNR was more rhetorical than real. It remained a small elitist group oriented to the immediate occupancy of power positions. The MNR fanned social conflict rhetorically but did little in the way of forging organizational links to a mass support base. In contrast, the Partido Izquierdista Revolucionario (PIR), a descendant of the revolutionary Marxist-socialist tendency of the youth movement of the late 1920's, assiduously sought an organized mass base, particularly among workers, lower middle-class teachers, and to some extent peasants. Following the Marxist-Leninist path, the PIR projected and prepared for a general revolution from below. It demanded both nationalization of the mines and agrarian reform. That the labor movement had a national political aim at all was due to the PIR. The PIR and the MNR were the two most potent tendencies at that time, the PIR forming a mass-oriented revolutionary counter-elite, the MNR forming a non-mass-oriented reformist counter-elite.

The MNR supplemented its parliamentary maneuvering with behind-the-scenes plotting with its former military allies—in particular, a secret society of young officers known as Razón de Patria (RADEPA). The plotting led to a successful coup in 1943, and the MNR was back in power under the auspices of a reform military government. This experiment, which followed the lines laid down by Davíd Toro and Germán Busch, was headed by Major Gualberto Villarroel. It lasted until July 1946, when a new status quo elite front, buttressed by the PIR and known as the antifascist front, led a coup that ended with Villarroel hanging from a lamppost with a rope about his neck.

During Villarroel's tenure the MNR, following Toro's lead in seeking to control mass bases from above, began building, for the first time, state-sponsored links with the working-class groups. Of particular importance was the formation under MNR sponsorship in 1944 of the Federación Sindical de Trabajadores Mineros de Bolivia (FSTMB). The leader of the new miners' group was a political unknown, Juan Lechín Oquendo. The statist labor policy (often called Peronist) of the MNR brought it into a violent clash with the PIR. MNR suppression and violence was one of the factors that pushed the PIR into the status quo elite antifascist front, formed in the 1940's.

In 1945 in La Paz, Villarroel convened the first national Indian conference—the first time that a national government had attacked the general problem of agrarian relations and the question of the status of the Indian peasant. But the conference did not attack the question of agrarian reform and produced only two decrees, one abolishing personal services and the other unpaid labor services. After Villarroel's fall, neither decree was obeyed or enforced. The congress was important, however, in that it had seriously considered the Indian question, stimulated peasant organization, and brought the MNR into some contact with peasant groups.

THE MNR: FROM PARTY TO MOVEMENT

The period from July 1946 to April 1952 is known in MNR lore as the *sexenio*. With Villarroel's fall, the bulk of the MNR's top leadership was driven into exile, and the second rank was forced to go underground. There began in the party a heated postmortem debate on future tactics. One group, led by Rafael Otazo, wanted to de-escalate conflict and seek accommodations with the restored status quo elite; another, led by Víctor Paz Estenssoro, argued for radicalizing the situation and building for the first time a truly organized mass base. By 1947 the Paz line had won and the party entered a period of self-transformation, from an elitist cabal to a mass-based revolutionary movement. For most party leaders, however, the transformation reflected a change in tactics rather than orientation. They sought to broaden the party's base in the urban middle-class and artisan groups, in the *clase popular*, and in the labor movement.[12]

The party had considerable success with the first two groups. A nationwide underground organization was formed. The movement adopted a cellular structure with essentially three levels: neighborhood cells, local and regional *"comandos,"* and a national political committee. The organization was poorly coordinated, however. The national political committee was isolated in La Paz, where it organized local commandos and cells, while groups in other areas had to function pretty much on their own. This primary party system, led by former second-level party leaders, was restricted almost completely to urban areas and comprised mainly middle-class, *clase popular*, and some artisan elements.

The party's relations with the labor movement were exceedingly complex. The MNR came to the labor movement late. While far from unified, the movement had an independent history, its own organizations, and—what is more important—its own emergent sectoral elite. The movement's previous political connections were mainly with the Left, which while not co-opting labor, provided the slogans and the ideological and rhetorical framework through which the movement emerged to political maturity. Thus, by 1947 the labor groups, especially the railway workers and miners, while favorably disposed toward the MNR because of its previous reformist efforts, were independently organized and led, and had an essentially revolutionary socialist orientation. In addition, there existed among labor leaders more than a little distrust of bourgeois politicians, no matter how radical their rhetoric.[13]

The MNR's entry into the labor movement was facilitated when the Partida Izquierdista Revolucionario (PIR), by participating in openly antilabor governments after 1946, was completely discredited. The demise of the PIR, however, did not leave a clear field to the MNR. Between 1940 and 1946, the smaller Trotskyite Party, Partido Obrero Revolucionario (POR), had successfully infiltrated the unions, especially in the mines. During the period of MNR reorganization (1946–47), Juan Lechín Oquendo, nominally an *MNRista*, had drawn quite close to the POR union cadres. The POR's influence became clear when, in 1946, Guillermo Lora, a POR chieftain, drafted a statement which was adopted by the FSTMB and sanctioned by Lechín. The statement, known as *La*

Tesis de Pulacayo, was more radical than anything the MNR ever posted and was in conflict with the MNR position on a number of basic points.[14]

The upshot was that the MNR never directly co-opted labor into the party. For the individual worker, the local syndicate and the functional federation were the most important points of organization. These units were, in the main, either controlled or influenced by *PORistas* and *PIRistas*. More and more, the MNR came to represent labor politically, but as an ally in a fight rather than a formulator of labor's goals.

The party then broadened its base but tended to split into two allied but separate groupings. The primary party organization directly incorporated middle-class and other previously unorganized groups, the labor Left section had its own organization. Although willing to work together, relations between the two branches were considerably strained. The primary organization retained the original MNR middle-class reformist outlook and contemplated the labor Left's emerging power with a suspicion which was returned by the Left. Both groups assiduously maintained their autonomy. The Lechín group exercised control over the choice of labor electoral candidates, and the national political committee showed its distrust by not assigning Lechín to an important national post until late in the 1946–52 period.[15] In addition, the old MNR leadership continually sought to use its old coup formula by plotting with military groups and the cryptofascist Falange Socialista Boliviana (FSB). In short, the primary leaders were willing to use labor but did not want to see its power grow; they preferred to take power with a minimum of labor assistance.

Bitter resistance by the status quo elite soon made it clear that the MNR would not soon return to power by means of a simple coup. More and more the party was forced to rely on a mass-based thrust, and Lechín's labor Left pivot became more powerful. The growing power of labor became apparent in the 1951 elections. The MNR, in covert alliance with a new Communist party, entered the fray with a platform promising universal suffrage, nationalization, and agrarian reform.[16] The MNR won the elections, but with a plurality rather than the majority required by the constitution. Before the election could be decided by the congress, a military junta took power in the name of order, anti-Communism, and anti-fascism.

The MNR's 1951 showing demonstrated that it was the strongest single counter-system force. There occurred, as a result, a classic bandwagon effect. From both left and right counter-elite groups either openly defected to the MNR or sought its cooperation. Of the new adherents, many more came from the Left than from the Right. Lechín's labor Left axis swelled, shifting the internal party balance in his favor. The new left supporters lined up behind Lechín with the avowed purpose of using the MNR to achieve victory and then to radicalize it from within. The Left's position was buttressed further by a new generation of students who flocked to the MNR but identified with the revolutionary Left more than with the old reformist Right.

The right-left division in the party worsened. The exile leadership under Paz Estenssoro took essentially a pragmatic position aimed at fashioning the most effective instrument possible.

MNR's connections with the peasants were even less direct than with labor. During this period there was some communication between peasant organizations and the national parties bidding for their support, but the peasants generally kept their distance and avoided direct commitments. The situation was further complicated by the MNR right wing, which included some medium-sized landholders and provincial bourgeoisie, who, while hospitable to the involvement of the miners, feared any mobilization of the peasants which might lead to profound changes in the countryside.[17] As a result, the MNR did not form any real alliances with peasant organizations until after the revolution. Up to 1952, the MNR was primarily a movement born of, and primarily aimed at, the tin-based national system.

THE INSURRECTION AND REVOLUTION

The uprising of Easter Week, 1952, began in classical coup fashion. Elements of the MNR, in conjunction with the national police led by General Seleme, minister of government in the junta, began the action on April 9. The scenario envisioned a Villarroel model—an alliance of the MNR, dissident military elements, and the police, with Seleme as president. By the end of the first day, however, key units of the army rallied to the government, and the uprising floundered. Seleme deserted the cause and sought asylum. MNR irregular units fought on and by midday on April 11 were joined by armed railway and factory workers. The tide turned decisively when armed miners seized a munitions train above La Paz and surrounded potential reinforcements in the city of Oruro. On the same day, in the face of growing civil resistance, the military crumbled and the MNR took the government. Contrary to plan, the MNR, which had come to power without military support, was now reliant primarily on its armed working-class allies.

The tension between the reformist-oriented MNR primary group and the more revolutionary labor Left came immediately to the surface. The big question was which position the exile leaders, particularly Paz, would adopt. In anticipation of Paz's return, the Right dug into the national administrative apparatus. The Left set out to organize its mass base. Within days a fairly coherent system of workers' militia was in operation and a national labor confederation, Central Obrera Boliviana (COB), was established under Lechín's leadership. The COB demanded and received "co-government." Under this theory, the COB was recognized as the only legitimate voice of Bolivian labor and was given the right to name the occupants of the key government ministries of mines and petroleum (new), peasant affairs (new), and labor (old). Paz returned on April 17 and was greeted by a massive COB-staged rally, which demanded nationalization, agrarian reform, and the vote. In the ensuing weeks the COB continued to bring massive public pressure on official decision-makers.

In the face of these conflicting trends, Paz and a number of other top leaders adopted what can be called a pragmatic nationalist position. They were willing to bow to demonstrable power but sought to keep it within a national development movement headed by the MNR. The result was that in gauging power realities, Paz moved left, and a Center-Left coalition began to emerge. Paz pursued the coalition, not simply because of the COB's power, but also because he needed labor support to ward off potential counter-revolutionary blows and because he sought to neutralize the *COBistas* of the more radical Left, who urged pushing aside the bourgeois MNR. He showed himself willing to bend to pressure from the Left, but at the same time sought to co-opt and eventually neutralize it.

With varying degrees of resistance, the Right either opposed completely or sought major modifications in what are now considered the four revolutionary achievements of the MNR: (1) universal suffrage, (2) downgrading of the military, (3) nationalization of the big three tin companies, and (4) agrarian reform. The Right gave way before the Center-Left on the first three measures, but gained concessions that made the measures tolerable. Not all tin, for example, was nationalized, and the measure was presented as a blow against the big three, not against private property as such. With Center support, the line was also held on the demands of the Left for total destruction of the army. The institution was saved by reducing manpower, by a drastic budget cut, by a purge of the officer corps, and by a redefinition of the army's function to one of providing technical and organizational support for development programs.

The Left did not get all it wanted, but its gains were major. The downgrading of the army heightened the power of the militias, the bulk of which, while nominally MNR-directed, were really under COB control. The concept of "co-government" was broadened so as to include the mines, where the FSTMB was given the right of *control obrero*, that is, participation in management decisions with the right of veto. The power drift was clearly to the labor Left.

The issue that really wracked the party was agrarian reform. On this issue the Right stiffened considerably, and the struggle dragged on throughout the summer and fall of 1952. In the late fall a new variable was introduced. Sporadically at first, then almost daily, reports reached La Paz of peasant uprisings and land seizures in the Cochabamba Valley. By December, the uprisings had spread to the departments of La Paz, Oruro, and Sucre.

The origins of the peasant movement are not of concern here. Suffice it to note that the labor Left encouraged the movement. Through the COB and the ministry of peasant affairs, the peasants were encouraged to organize unions and seize the land. The Right demanded that the government stem the movement. The official party adopted first a highly equivocal position, and then seemed to support the peasant drive. On January 6, 1953, a number of original party leaders in conjunction with army and police officers staged a coup that fizzled almost as soon as it began. On January 7, the COB militia poured into La Paz demanding right wing heads. Given little choice, Paz Estenssoro began to purge the Right. It was a most mild purge. The known leaders were exiled but no blood was shed and the complicity of many was covered up. The Center clearly did not wish to be totally reliant on the Left.

On January 20, a commission, which included ex-*PIRistas* and ex-*PORistas* was called together and charged with drafting an agrarian reform measure. Peasant uprisings continued throughout the winter and spring. On August 3, 1953, agrarian reform was promulgated in a document that projected the reform as a development measure and was full of the best economic theorizings, but it was clear that in heavily populated key areas, such as the Cochabamba Valley and the Lake Titicaca region, the document merely ratified a *fait accompli*. In the meantime, well-organized and armed peasant unions were formed throughout the country.

POLITICAL DIMENSIONS: 1953–60

For purposes of analysis, it is convenient to study the post-1952 process from the perspective of the MNR core elite, which I have dubbed the pragmatic nationalist Center. The group's history goes back to the original formation of the party. From the beginning, this group saw itself as the vanguard of a new Bolivia. Rightly or wrongly, its members saw themselves as "developers." They thought mainly in terms of economic categories and projected their notion of a modern Bolivian nation state in terms of seizing and using state power to direct economic growth. Originally, they operated on a basis of piecemeal reform; only later did they become revolutionaries; they were at best reluctant revolutionaries.

By mid-1953 the MNR core had presided over (rather than directed) a profound drama of revolutionary destruction and now faced a most troublesome dilemma of revolutionary construction. From the point of view of its own basic goals, it must be concluded that the MNR failed in the task. Its failure is confirmed, not simply by the coup of 1964, which unseated the MNR, but by the fact that the task of redefining and reconstructing a coherent ongoing national state unit is still the key political and economic problem of Bolivia. In this sense the revolution continues.

Politically, the period from August 1953 to November 1964 can be broken into three periods. The first, from 1953 to 1956, was marked by the dominance of a Center-Left coalition. During this period the COB-led labor Left was in ascendance, and the FSTMB was the most potent single power group. Political initiative was out of MNR hands, and Paz and his coterie acted as a man on a runaway horse, who elects to hang on until his mount tires, rather than risk the danger of leaping off.

In early 1956, the remaining rightist elements and part of the MNR center again attempted to stem the left drive. They rallied around one of the major figures of the party, Walter Guevara Arze. The Left-dominated party congress fought off the Guevara challenge but accepted an internal compromise, engineered by Paz in the name of party unity. Under the compromise, the party's number-two man, Hernán Siles, generally considered of rightist sentiments, was chosen as presidential candidate. The Left received the vice-presidency and controlled the drafting of the party's legislative candidate lists.

The second period, 1956–60, began with the elections of 1956. Although the MNR swept the elections, there was one most disturbing sign: The cities voted heavily for the Falange Socialista Boliviana, now the major rallying point of counter-revolutionary sentiment. The portent was clear. The MNR, orginally a middle-class party had lost middle-class support. Factors in the middle-class defection were the dominance of labor, a new round of inflation that reached crisis proportions, and fear of the emerging peasant masses.[18]

Under Siles, power within the party shifted from the Center-Left to the Center-Right. He ousted Left members from party posts, rehabilitated many of the figures of January 6, 1953, and purged the legislative lists in the 1958 elections, ending the Left majority. In addition, he split the COB by playing on internal clashes of interests and principles. Lechín's hard-core Left fell back on the FSTMB and the miners' militia. Siles further wooed the middle class by stemming the inflation and by taking the pressure off right groups such as the Falange Socialista Boliviana. Most importantly, he began to rebuild the army as a counterweight to the miners' militia and openly courted the *campesinos*, turning the Cochabamba units against the miners.[19]

The four years of Siles' presidency were marked by bitter clashes between his Center-Right coalition and the supporters of Lechín. The clashes were marked by strikes and violence. In 1959 Siles, unwilling to split the party, backed off his anti-Left push. There emerged a standoff and stabilization of power which amounted to political immobilism. An enervating torpor settled over the country as the various sides watched for the first hostile moves of the others.

In preparation for the elections of 1960, another compromise was concluded. Paz returned to run for president with Lechín as his running mate. The Left perceived the solution as a victory and began to talk of 1964 and Lechín's presidency. The party Right shared this view, and as a result, following Guevara Arze's lead, bolted the party and formed a rival party, the Movimiento Nacionalista Revolucionario Auténtico (MNRA).

POLITICS VS. ECONOMICS: THE QUESTION OF SOCIAL COSTS

Before analyzing the critical third period beginning in 1960, it would be useful to summarize the highlights of the economic situation in the first two periods and then consider some of the tensions between the political and economic dimensions of the situation.

The basic trend of the economic picture was simple: Rather than develop economically, the country went into an economic tailspin. The three major features of the tailspin were: (1) a 20 percent drop in estimated per capita income between 1952 and 1958, (2) runaway inflation, and (3) the deterioration of the state mining corporation, Corporación Minera de Bolivia (COMIBOL), to the point where it was losing over $15 million a year by 1962. In addition, there was a precipitous decline in agricultural production and an exhaustion of hard monetary reserves.[20]

The position of COMIBOL was central to the overall picture of deterioration if for no other reason than because tin remained the basis of the developed portion of the economy. Not the least of COMIBOL's problems was a factor clearly out of the hands of the revolutionary government. In the first instance, available ore was simply used up, and plants and equipment remained old and inefficient. By all odds it was a questionable prize that the revolutionaries had seized. Secondly, the termination of the Korean War led to a steady drop in the world price of tin.

Yet there were aspects undoubtedly related to the revolution and the policies of the MNR regime. It will be recalled that one of the keystones of the MNR's development image from its earliest days was a program of economic diversification. True to its goal and its pre-1952 conception of how to pursue it, the government sought to diversify in three areas: agriculture, especially in the east; oil; and infrastructure. From the earliest days the MNR had held that the lack of diversification was due to the nonnational utilization of tin profits. Under both Busch and Villarroel, measures had been taken in an attempt to give the government control of the exchange earned by tin. The purpose was to use the exchange to sponsor diversification through the state development agency created by Busch. It was firmly believed that capital for diversification would come from tin. The revolutionary government implemented this belief by the the age old inflationary methods of borrowing and printing paper money. By manipulation of multiple exchange rates, COMIBOL was forced to sustain a heavy loss in exchange transactions. In effect, the government was systematically decapitalizing COMIBOL.[21]

Deeply involved with COMIBOL's problem and the entire economic problem was another governmental problem which can be described as "payoff." The MNR mobilized its mass base—particularly labor—between 1946 and 1952 by expressing the frustrated demands of these groups. Those demands arose out of a desire for concrete economic betterment. The MNR came to power with a large debt. Its support groups immediately began to cash in their IOU's. The attempt to meet this debt on the part of the MNR meant a major process of income redistribution and an overall increase in consumption. This spurt of consumption aggravated the problem of capital accumulation and accelerated the inflationary process.

The sector to benefit most immediately from the redistribution and consumption was labor, with tighter control of working hours, wage increases, bonuses, social benefits, and many other advantages. Within the labor sector the miners scored the greatest apparent gains. Thousands of miners laid off after 1946 were rehired, and in all enterprises it became virtually impossible to fire or lay off. Labor's new position was further strengthened by the imposition of rent controls and by *pulperías* selling subsidized articles. All of these factors added up to a tremendous capital outlay for the government and society at large, especially in relation to the meager available surplus.[22]

The peasants obviously benefited greatly, although this was more difficult to measure. No doubt one of the factors behind the drop in agricultural production was a rise in peasant subsistence consumption. There were widespread reports of peasant decimation of *hacienda* live stock and other forms of consumption of rural capital. Since they lived primarily on a subsistence level, peasants, on the whole, were protected from the more pernicious effects of the inflation, and by being sellers in a high-price market certain rural areas directly benefited from the inflation. The issue of peasant gains is quite hard to measure, but certain authoritative sources are of the opinion that the real long-range gainer of the redistribution process was the peasant.[23]

By 1956 the issue that overrode all issues was inflation. The Bolivian inflation not only debilitated the national economy but gnawed away at the delicate sociopsychological framework of the country. The first evidence of damage was in the popular support of the MNR. The wild fluctuation of money poisoned the tone of public life, banished predictability from sociopolitical relations, and brought insecurity to all sectors of the society. The inflation became a form of social war, of each against all. He who could not muster political power on a personal or sectoral basis was a loser. In Bolivia that meant the disorganized urban middle stratum. Thus the middle class, which supported the MNR because of inflation in the old regime, now turned against it because of an even more serious inflation under the revolutionary regime.

The Siles administration (1956–60) devoted almost all of its energies to stemming the inflation. The president's attack included demands that labor accept wage freezes and give up the gains it had wrested from the Paz government to protect its position. A large section of the COB, led by Lechín, interpreted this action as a demand by the petite bourgeoisie that labor give up its rightful claims to a better existence—claims that had been legitimized by labor's role in the uprising of 1952. Out of this clash issued the right-left battle, which ended in a stalemate. The nature of the stalemate was such, however, that labor's commitment to the MNR was deeply shaken, and, while the opposition of the urban middle was muted, it continued to view the MNR with hostility.

Bolivia was unfortunately drawn into one of those political and economic vicious circles so common to underdeveloped countries. The inflation was partly a result of internal fissures in Bolivian society and in the MNR itself. The long-lived inflation increased the fissures and politically alienated important groups. Attempts to alleviate the inflation only drove in more wedges and alienated important groups, particularly the miners. The small fund of community feeling that had been generated by the common effort of insurrection was shattered by the post-1952 inflation. Each sector of society looked on every other sector as a potential threat to itself and watched the MNR government suspiciously for any sign of favoritism.

THE CLOSING OF THE VICIOUS CIRCLE

Rapid, state-sponsored economic development presupposes the central creation and direction of power and is, therefore, in the most fundamental sense political.[24] This simple fact was especially apparent in Bolivia, for on the other side of the coin of economic retrogression was a general breakdown of the ability of national institutions to direct the country. The issue was one of internal sovereignty, that is, the ability of a central authoritative decision center effectively to overrule local nonauthoritative centers.

Insurrections such as that which the MNR carried out in 1952 are often referred to as a seizure of power. This label is a misnomer. Successful revolutions such as the MNR's do not result in the seizure of power, they destroy power—or, as is more often the case, confirm its previous demise. Downgrading of the army, nationalization, and the agrarian reform were extensions of this process of destroying the institutionalization of power which, in Bolivia, was the old regime. Upon destruction, power does not immediately reappear at the same level but tends to diffuse itself from abstract "national" centers to more concrete local and segmental centers. The task of making a modern national development revolution hinges on the ability to reassemble and reinstitutionalize power at the abstract national level.

The first task facing the modern revolutionary elite—in a field of competing revolutionary elites—is to establish the effective sovereignty and ultimate authority of a decision center. Because the MNR sought national development, sovereignty meant authoritative control over the entire unit, whereas in pre-1952 Bolivia the vast localized agrarian system was irrelevant to the tin-based government. Indeed it was the effectively nonnational character of the Bolivian state that the revolutionary generation discovered in the trenches of the Chaco.

Bolivia's dismal performance in the field of economic development, despite the avowed goal of the MNR revolutionaries, was due to the failure of the MNR elite to solve the internal problem of national sovereignty. Holding office but not effectively governing Bolivia, the MNR elite was incapable of mobilizing the country's human and material resources for the attainment of its goals. Under the MNR, national institutions became epiphenomenal to the forces which actually held sway. The stagnation and immobility that gripped revolutionary Bolivia were due to the kinds of informal structures that emerged.

Through its revolutionary measures, the MNR pushed aside the only class of national breadth Bolivia had known. The MNR elite of middle-class and déclassé intellectuals was a product of the urban tin system and hence not really a nationwide elite; it was a thin, sectorally based elite. The core support of this thin elite, both psychologically and organizationally, was the equally thin and nonnational urban middle sectors. Very soon after 1952, a sector of the core elite was pushed out of the party. Shortly thereafter, the party's main public support turned to the active opposition. With these developments, the core MNR elite of would-be nation builders found itself in a most peculiar position. On the surface, Bolivia was functioning like any other single-party state. Beneath the surface, a very narrow middle-class intellectual elite occupied official national positions, but their continued stay in office depended upon the support of two autonomous, organized, and armed sectors (peasants and workers), over whom they had little or no direct control.

Of particular importance was the question of the ability to use force. As Max Weber pointed out, one of the hallmarks of the modern state is a legitimate monopoly of the ability to use force. The importance of this characteristic does not lie simply in the ultimate ability of the state to back its commands by force, but in the fact that private force is no longer the only means of reconciling disputes among the various parts of the unit. A revolutionary situation—one that continues beyond an insurrection—is a situation in which force tends to become the most prevalent means of settling conflicts. In such a situation "naked force must remain the argument of the last resort, and the distribution of military might the principal determinant of social structure."[25] Many theorists and practitioners of revolution have shown that the old regime fails in the end when its military crumbles internally. This was surely the case in Bolivia, where corruption, poor morale, and intrigue rendered the military incapable of defeating a relatively weak civilian force.

The relevance of force does not end with the defeat of the old regime. If anything, force becomes more relevant. As pointed out above, the post-1952 inflation originated in division over questions of redistribution and in time worsened the situation. Bolivia experienced a state of protracted war, and the question of force became even more relevant in determining structures and process.

Almost immediately after the insurrection, the formal state, now represented by the MNR, lost its legitimate monopoly of force.

Force at first passed to the populace at large. Very quickly, however, it passed at intermediate regional and sectoral levels to militias and private armies. Although on paper they were part of the MNR, the militias, aside from a few specific party units, were not controlled by the party elite. The powerful workers' militias were organized under the COB, which declared itself a semisovereign body, with autonomous state-like jurisdiction. Actually the COB's hold on the militias was tenuous; real control was lodged at the lower levels in functional federations and specific factories or camps.

The same process was repeated in the rural areas. The first political effects of the agrarian reform were extreme atomization and the breaking of rural control. Lacking any organizational links to the peasant masses, the MNR government could not step into the void—nor could the COB, for that matter.[26]

In many parts of the country the peasants simply withdrew from the national existence into an atomized state. In other regions, the peasants were united (often by force) into regional federations dominated by powerful unions. This regional consolidation of peasant power was particularly marked in the area around Lake Titicaca and in the now famous Cochabamba Valley. These two areas were brought under the personal domination of two caciques: Toribio Salas on the Altiplano and José Rojas Guevara in the valley. Both leaders constantly had to fight threats from local challengers and to struggle with each other for control of the national peasant confederation. Agricultural Bolivia was characterized by a bewildering array of patterns of local authority and power, punctuated by intra- and inter-regional violence.

The devolution of force (and hence effective power) did not stop there. In pre-revolutionary Bolivia, the geographical bulk of the country was even less connected to the state than the *hacienda*-based rural system. The great semitropical area known as the Oriente, which encompassed the Departments of Pando, Beni, and

Santa Cruz, maintained almost no national connections, a fact brought home by the Chaco War. The MNR had no real links to these areas before the insurrection and was in no position to establish any after 1952. Here again, the ability to use force was lost at the state level and consolidated locally under personal strongmen. Great chunks of these rich areas were brought under the domination of two major individuals: Rubén Julio Castro, whose realm stretched across the Beni and Pando, and Luís Sandoval Morón, who subjugated Santa Cruz. Nominally members of the MNR, these men were in reality autonomous territorial rulers not unlike the early nineteenth-century *caudillos*. The ruled through private armies and quite often battled each other in order to extend their territorial bases.

In post-1952 Bolivia, a number of dynamic processes were taking place. The most basic process was mobilization. Through revolutionary action, previously excluded groups emerged as political determinants. As a result, there was a precipitous increase in the quantity and quality of the demands made on the meager resources available for distribution. Immediately after the insurrection, the accumulated wealth was redistributed to the benefit, mainly, of peasants and workers. When the original surplus was gone, the support publics of the revolution began to struggle among themselves, more over the question of protecting gains and distributing losses than over new gains. The presumed commonality of interests of the tri-class movement was contradicted by revolutionary reality, and party unity at both the elite and public level disappeared.

It was this reality that the thin MNR core had to face in its attempt to establish the authority of its government and the legitimacy of its particular image of a new, developed Bolivia. Complicating the situation was a development logic which, in that situation, demanded that consumption be deferred in favor of investment.

During the 1953–56 period the MNR government attempted to

meet consumption and investment demands at the same time. The result was a vicious circle of inflation that further eroded internal unity. During this period the social costs of the dual policy were largely borne by the urban middle class. At the official national level, a power alliance of the old MNR core and the labor-based Left sector elite held sway. The general trend was toward some form of state socialism. Under Siles the inflation was stemmed, and the then dominant power coalition, with its Left trend, reversed. The attempt was to establish some form of state-sponsored capitalism enforced by an MNR center-Right elite power alliance. Social costs were shifted back onto labor. But while stemming the Left drive, Siles was unable to establish a trend toward the original MNR model. His regime ended in a stalemate characterized by political and economic immobilism.[27]

Behind the immobilism was the continuing clash of economic and political logic, the dual question of elite control and social costs, the continuing process of national power deflation, and the establishment of independent nonnational power centers. Despite early trends, by 1960 neither the question of control nor that of social costs had been resolved in any effective manner.

From the perspective of the MNR pragmatic center, which gave a kind of continuity at the national level during this confused period, the gut issue was how to generate political support while fomenting development. To generate political support, the MNR core had to rely on the mechanism of demand satisfaction. They were forced to buy loyalty and compliance. There developed a complex market system in which support for national leadership became a negotiated item, with immediate concrete rewards as the medium of exchange. As the situation unfolded, however, it became apparent that local and segmental nonauthoritative organizations were growing stronger, while the national authoritative center was growing weaker.[28]

In post-1952 Bolivia the pattern of interactions was such that the thin MNR national elite was able to generate only enough support for the contingent occupancy of office, but not enough to launch development programs which would divert resources from demand satisfaction. Potential development energies and resources were consistently diverted, resulting in an all too common vicious circle of underdevelopment. The political manifestation of this vicious circle was an increase in the dispersal of power to local centers, increasing social gaps both horizontally between groups and vertically between groups and national structures, and causing increased social conflict and political instability.[29]

The MNR national government ended by reacting now to this thrust, now to that. The party functioned not according to traditional Western theories of democracy (as the connecting link between government and populace) nor according to the modern theory that describes parties in the new one-party states as mechanisms for mobilizing support for government initiative. Rather the party became an instrument through which various sectors could legitimately assault the system's meager collective surplus. The party came to have little or no control over its constituent parts, and as a result both party and government became captives of shifting local and segmental power combinations. Relevant forms of power were reduced in the main to direct control over sectors of the economy and ultimately to the capacity to threaten the government with autonomous force. Beneath the single-party veneer was a society in a state of incipient civil war.

Forced by the situation to rely on demand satisfaction, but lacking a resource base capable of meeting fully the demands made on it, the various MNR governments had to maintain themselves through a complex process of robbing Peter to pay Paul. It was a self-defeating process which, while it allowed the government to cling precariously to the symbols of political power, blocked any real national development by draining the country's already limited capital resource base as well as most of the capital which entered in the form of foreign aid. Similarly, the political aim of gaining a solid base of support was in the end negated. The nature of the agrarian reform, the increased demands, the maintenance of subsidized stores, all ate deeply into the country's economic capacity. At the same time the devolution of power, authority, and status to some groups at the expense of others bit into the country's limited psychological capital.

During most of the MNR's reign, this process was institutionalized as a style of public life. Organizations proliferated, as each sector sought to build a solid front with which to protect what it had, while it assaulted the system for more. The MNR itself proliferated into factions (and into factions within factions), through which each group sought a legitimate "in" at the national level. When this mechanism for pressing demands failed to be effective, the weakened group resorted to strikes, work stoppages, or partial uprisings. Thus the system was continually in a state of crisis.

Under Siles, this process became so institutionalized that it won a kind of acceptance in some sectors. Alone, no single sector could take over, and by this time no group trusted another enough to enter into a permanent alliance. Rather than risk all by rupturing the circle, most groups either actively perpetuated it, or did so by default. The myth of the national revolution and its popular instrument, the MNR, was strengthened; deals and counter-deals were made and broken.

The fact was that no single group was strong enough to seize the government. The degree of fragmentation was such that no group had enough faith in any other group to enter into an effective power alliance. Yet many groups were strong enough to veto actions which threatened their interests. The result was a power standoff, an immobilized government, and continual consumption of the country's resource base. For four years a power alliance had functioned, but under Siles it was upset. His new alliance did not (or could not) impose a solution—hence the immobilism which greeted Paz Estenssoro on his return to office in 1960.

TO BREAK THE CIRCLE

The reelection of Paz Estenssoro coincided with the election of John F. Kennedy to the presidency of the United States. In launching his Alliance for Progress Kennedy was looking for a showcase of "democratic revolutions," whereas Paz was looking for the political and economic means to help Bolivia to break out of its immobilism. The two aims converged: From Kennedy, Paz received a commitment of support in exchange for the adoption by Bolivia of the implied sociopolitical model of the Alliance. The decision was not difficult for Paz; the Alliance was quite hospitable to many of the MNR's future projections.

Paz made it clear that above all else his government would seek economic development. In an early speech he made development the ultimate standard of measurement of the revolution. Indeed he redefined the very concept of a counter-revolutionary. Henceforth a counter-revolutionary would be one who stood in the way of development, the clear implication being that the major counter-revolutionary forces were labor and the COB.[30]

On the basis of the analysis of COMIBOL's problems in 1956 by the Ford, Bacon, and Davis firm and the analysis of the monetary situation in the U.S.-supported Eder report, all of Bolivia's economic problems were traced to labor—particularly the miners.[31] The miners, it was argued, were extraordinarily unproductive. The causes for this lack of productivity were (1) unrealistic wages and social services, (2) featherbedding, and (3) subsidized stores.

According to this argument, labor had to be brought into line with productivity, and labor demands had to be deferred. Given labor's political and managerial power, how could this be accomplished? Underlying the situation, it was argued, was labor's lack of discipline. First and foremost, labor would have to be disciplined and managerial authority reestablished. Since the key to the economy was the mines—the country's only source of capital—the first labor group to be "disciplined" was the miners. Paz Estenssoro accepted this argument and made it the basis of his government. Thus, despite the apparent return to the 1952–56 Center-Left coalition, Paz, backed by the U.S., put himself on a collision course with Lechín, the miners, and eventually the entire labor Left.

The economic linchpin of the Paz (U.S.) thrust was the so-called triangular plan for the tin industry, in which the United States, the International Monetary Fund, and the West German government promised capital, equipment, and know-how, while the Bolivian government promised a reduced work force, a disciplined labor body, and governmental authority.

The political component of the Paz thrust, therefore, had to be an attempt to break the immobilized standoff described above, and the assertion of internal national sovereignty. Obviously this was a difficult and politically dangerous task. In the immobilized system internal conflict was kept within bounds by the unwillingness of any sector to risk half a loaf by breaking the system and forcing alliances against it.[32] Now, by attempting to break the system from above, Paz renewed intense internal conflicts and forced groups to find defensive alliances where they might.

The base of Paz's strategy was to forge a working power coalition capable of imposing the new course on Bolivia. The strategy operated at three levels. The first was regional. Here the aim was to assert national authority in all regions or at least to ensure that regional bosses were loyal to the government. Hence he sought to break the power of Luís Sandoval Morón by supporting Rubén

Julio Castro, while simultaneously declaring Santa Cruz a military zone and putting it under a military governor. He also intervened in the Cochabamba Valley's intra-*campesino* war and helped Rojas consolidate his control.[33] Finally, on the Altiplano, by attempting to put men loyal to him in control of the region, he sponsored challengers to the pro-COB Salas.

The second level was national. The key factor here was the attempt to reassert the state's ability to use forceful sanctions. With U.S. aid, the army was rebuilt and retrained, its image refurbished, and its functions effectively increased. To the army's development services was added internal pacification, in which the army was used in the Cochabamba Valley and against Sandoval Morón in Santa Cruz. Unlike Siles, who had actually begun the army buildup, Paz did not seek allies among the party's old Right. Instead he sought out a whole new generation of young people, loyal to him and his goals. Finally, he sought to create a means to redirect the middle class and in effect to create a new middle-class technocratic elite. To accomplish this he established with U.S. help the Instituto Tecnológico Boliviano (ITB), independent of the university system and run on strict merit principles. In short, at the national level he was betting on (1) a new and theoretically modern-minded military, (2) a new generation of bright young men, and (3) a new generation of middle-class youth, liberated from the status values of their parents.

On the third level, between the national and territorial levels, the pivotal issue was intersectoral power and a popular base of support for the regime. Here Paz sought to reorient the revolution, from a previous identification with labor to an identification with the peasant masses. He sought to convince the *campesinos* that the revolution was their revolution, that his aims were identical with theirs, and that his enemies were theirs. At the same time he attempted to meet the demands of *campesino* groups and of general rural investment. He also made clear that bettering the situation depended on spurring development and controlling the Communists (i.e., the COB and the FSTMB).

In the light of the previous discussion of demands and supports, Paz's strategy appears to have been: (1) to win more solid peasant support by guaranteeing peasant demands at the expense of other groups, especially the miners; (2) to reassert the national ability to exercise forceful sanctions by rebuilding and modernizing the military; and (3) to break the power of other groups and to stimulate state-sponsored development through a policy of selective demand satisfaction and a selective application of force where necessary.

The Paz post-1960 strategy was based on a social image that lay deep in MNR thinking. In recent years, the image has often been expressed in the concept *sociedad democrática burgesa*. This concept envisions a dynamic society governed by a progressive middle-class elite, which would use the state, not to destroy capitalism, but to regulate it for the sake of national growth. The image, especially in its most recent variation under Paz, coincides closely with the development model which the Brazilian political-sociologist Helio Jaguaribe terms *capitalismo del estado*.[34] This image differs from that of the labor Left, whose societal image is more analogous to the model Jaguaribe terms *socialismo desarrollista*. In the general Latin American context, the first Bolivian model harked back to Mexico, while the second in many respects anticipated Cuba.

The second model envisioned an eventual predominance of the labor Left elite, socialization of the means of production, and the abolition of a market system. Throughout this process, labor and peasant consumption demands would be met at the cost of the former upper and middle groups. The two models were fundamentally incompatible, especially when one considers the reaction of the United States to a *Fidelista* Cuba.

Central to the problem confronting Paz as he moved against the labor Left was the fact that, as Jaguaribe argues, the *capitalismo del estado* model assumes an elite sprung from *la clase media tecno-crática.*[35] The reality of the situation was that the Bolivian middle stratum in general—and the MNR elite in particular—was not a technocratic stratum but rather a traditional *empleado*, or office-oriented bureaucratic stratum, which sought to imitate the traditional aristocratic upper stratum's life style. This point is critical to an understanding of the conflict situation, which Paz encountered after 1960.

The Instituto Tecnológico Boliviano (ITB), built with U.S. funds, was perceived as a threat by middle-class Bolivia, especially professors and students. As a result, the university emerged as a bastion of anti-Paz activity. It is by no means a coincidence that, on the day Paz fell, university students invaded the ITB and rein-corporated it into the autonomous university system. Since that day, many report that the standards and quality of technical education have declined sharply. The social values implicit in a modern technocratic image were fundamentally hostile to those of the traditional Bolivian middle life style and competitive situation, which included an all but guaranteed university degree.

This problem was particularly severe in the MNR. Unlike many other single-party regimes, the MNR never established strict criteria for party membership. Aside from the mild purge of 1953, there had been no systematic expulsion of party sectors, and most of those expelled in 1953 had found their way back under Siles.[36] The seeming omnipotence of the party made it a magnet for job-seekers who were willing to pay the price of a party oath for a government office. Thus the party grew year by year into a heterogeneous collection of persons whose loyalty to the party was mainly dependent on jobs. As the party expanded beyond the capacity of the society to generate bureaucratic roles, it began to disintegrate into factions, which, although they adopted ideological labels, were more often office-oriented cabals dedicated to the political fortunes of individuals.

Paz made it publicly clear that he saw the makeup of the party as a problem and that he intended to change it.[37] Actually, there was little he could do, and so for both technical and political reasons he eventually turned his back on the party and created his own cabal of loyal young men—many of post-1952 vintage. As a result, those excluded from this *camarilla* turned against him. Paz began to lose control of the party, and in the end was not really governing through the party at all.[38]

There is no space for a blow-by-blow account of how Paz and the MNR fell. The first major sign of disintegration appeared in 1960, when in fear of a new Paz-Lechín Center-Left alliance, a large section of the old Right followed Guevara Arze out of the party. As the multilevel strategy of Paz began to unfold in the early 1960's, all semblance of political cohesion and order began to give way. The most dramatic conflict was that between Paz and the labor Left, which reached a crisis in 1963, when the miners in Catavi Siglo XX seized seventeen hostages, including three American citizens. Significantly, the miners' rebellion crumbled when Paz mobilized against their camp a combined force of regular military and valley peasant units. Throughout the country, less dramatic signs of deterioration appeared daily.[39]

Paz's strategy forced group after group to turn against his regime. Territorial bosses like Sandoval Morón and Toribio Salas struggled to maintain their satrapies. Party members excluded from jobs, students, teachers, and the like began to conspire. A policy of wage freezes, layoffs, and termination of subsidized *pulperías* drove labor into the streets. In response, Paz declared his intention to smash a Communist threat; he abrogated "co-government," ignored *control obrero*, and sought to arrest key union leaders—actions which forced the bulk of the labor Left to mobilize behind Lechín, who had little choice but to turn against Paz if he was to retain his national prominence.

The outlook was not entirely negative. By forcing a break in the political immobilism, Paz also broke through the economic immobility. Important sectors of the economy, particularly agriculture, began to move and by 1965 Bolivia was registering a more than respectable yearly growth rate.[40] The possibility of continuing and generalizing the economic surge turned on Paz's ability to maintain his political thrust. Central to this ability were the military (which by 1964 was a small but cohesive and modernized force of about 10,000) and the organized sectors of the peasantry.

Under Paz, Bolivia was experiencing a historical reorientation comparable in magnitude to that occasioned by the liberals after 1898. As part of his attempt to develop and integrate a national reality, Paz was forcing the country to turn for the first time to the interior and to agriculture. The attempt to refurbish COMIBOL was more in the manner of removing what had become a debilitating obstacle to diversification and the move eastward, then a commitment of Bolivia's future to tin. As the country began to shift from the Altiplano and tin to the East and agriculture, the political capital of the miners declined and that of the peasants increased.

Seeing this shift, we can begin to grasp why the military (which many had counted out after 1952) emerged in the 1960's as the pivotal national institution. It was through the military that the national government achieved its first effective institutional presence in critical regions such as Santa Cruz. The military through its civic action program built roads, constructed schools, passed out food and equipment, and colonized land—all integral to the interior-directed development scheme. Finally, through the military the national center sought to establish a force capable of making its social cost allocation decisions stick and of eventually bringing local power to heel.

The importance of the peasant mass to this process is obvious. The Indian peasant was the critical human component of the shift; for it was the peasant who would wrench surplus from existing cultivated land and pioneer the opening of new land. Politically the peasant would provide the necessary mass support to ensure the legitimacy of the emergent regime. In the meantime peasant guns, supposedly loyal to the man who distributed the land, were being counted on to check any ambitions the military might develop.

The picture is that of a negative balance of power, forcibly altered in the 1960's into a situation in which power was suddenly fluid and in which a bewildering array of regional, segmented, and personal interests were compelled to fight for their metaphoric (and often their actual) lives—an environment characterized economically by such scarcities that the very need for development demanded the sacrifice of some interests, and characterized politically by a climate in which resolution of these conflicts more often than not turned on the will and the ability to use power in the form of force.

The situation was brought to a head in 1964 when Paz declared his intention of succeeding himself, an ambition which has occasioned more than one *golpe de estado* in Bolivian history. Previous to this declaration, embattled groups and individuals had found a rationale for relative restraint by planning to better their position at the end of Paz's term. This was particularly true of the Left, which since 1960 had been counting on Lechín's succeeding to the presidency in 1964. Paz's decision forced those suffering from his policies to contemplate the prospect of four more years of the same, not to mention the fact that in four years they might well be eliminated politically. They therefore had little choice but to seek Paz's elimination from the political scene.

Lechín was the first to make the break, announcing the creation of his own left party. Siles Suazo declared a hunger strike in protest against Paz's ambitions. The various non-MNR opposition groups on both Left and Right began to move. Throughout the country, an anti-Paz coalition began to form, composed of totally disparate ideological elements.

In the 1964 party convention, an event of particular significance occurred when the military forced Paz to jettison his hand-picked, officially nominated running mate for the popular head of the Air Force, General René Barrientos Ortuño. The Paz-Barrientos ticket won the elections easily, but it soon became apparent that large numbers of party members excluded from office in the new government were plotting with opposition groups. The situation became even more critical when Paz's own vice-president began to assail him openly, and the new minister of peasant affairs, José Rojas Guevara, identified himself with Barrientos.

In the fall of 1964, the final act of the drama was begun. The miners staged a violent uprising. Simultaneously, the national teachers' union took to the streets, demanding a major pay increase which the government, pleading the danger of inflation, refused to meet. In October the miners and teachers were joined by other workers and by secondary and university students. Barrientos repaired to Cochabamba and declared himself in rebellion. The government, besieged from within and without, called on the military and *campesinos* for help.

On November 3, key units of the army aligned themselves against the government. Paz again called for help from the peasants, but aside from a few Altiplano contingents, the legendary peasant masses did not materialize. Key leaders in the Cochabamba Valley, such as Rojas, Jorge Solís and Macedonio Juárez, had cast their lot with Barrientos and it was they, not the president, who controlled the allocation of peasant power.

Paz, on November 4, 1964, accepted the invitation of the army chief of staff, Alfredo Obando Candia, to depart for Lima and exile. With Paz gone, what was left of the MNR collapsed. Opposition groups maneuvered frantically to capture the government. In the confusion a brief comic opera was played out. On the evening of the fourth, Obando and Barrientos declared themselves co-presidents of Bolivia. Crowds assembled in the capital, demanding that Barrientos succeed to the presidency alone. Obando gave in, and Barrientos strode onto the balcony of the presidential palace to receive the accolades of the street mobs, but close behind the balcony windows stood Obando and the army.

The coup of November 1964 did not resolve any of the basic political or economic problems, unsolved since the revolution of 1952. The MNR has, for the moment at least, retired from the political field. Much to its chagrin, the labor Left found the governments of Barrientos and Obando more determined than that of Paz to break its control and to pile upon the shoulders of labor the burden of providing surpluses from the meager resources of Bolivia.[41] Hardest hit, thus far, is the miner—the man who for generations has scratched fortunes from the soil of Bolivia, but who, despite a revolution he helped to make, finds himself in 1967 a pariah, blamed for all the ills of his country.

The country as a whole still faces the problem of charting a new course, as it has since 1952, and of assembling a viable power coalition to make a new system effective. The logic of political support still clashes with the logic of primitive capital accumulation. The questions of control and social costs still await a workable solution. An awakened and mobilized populace continues to strain against an environment of extreme scarcity, and the demands for *mejoramiento*, born of that scarcity, continue to be heard by those elites who presume to govern and develop Bolivia.

CONCLUSION

The MNR of Bolivia is an example of what some authors have called "national popular movements."[42] Such movements are common to underdeveloped countries, including those of Latin America. It is argued that these movements constitute elite-led, cross-class alliances, formed to remove political obstacles to development. They are cross-class alliances because, in the underdeveloped context, it is not possible to achieve change through the classic single-class movements of Europe, such as a liberal, entrepreneurial, middle-class thrust or a socialist working-class thrust. Moreover, because of discontinuities in these societies such multiclass efforts are usually led by dissident sectors of the preexistent elite and/or sub-elite, directing the political energies of various popular groups.

The components of such movements, the argument continues, are brought into play by the variable impact of two factors: (1) the demonstration effect, and (2) local situations in which there are marked disparities between aspirations and outlets by which to realize them (status incongruence). Elites react mainly to the position of their country vis-à-vis the developed states and their reactions often are reinforced by a status problem arising out of the paucity of elite status roles in the local situation. Publics tend to react to the demonstrated popular consumption levels of the advanced states and to the denial of consumption in the local situation (frustration of expectations).

By the late 1920's the basic ingredients of a national popular movement were present in Bolivia. These factors derived from the skewed and eventually truncated pattern of development that Bolivia experienced between the 1880's and the 1920's. The new generation of elite and sub-elite youth faced a severe problem from lack of outlets and began to compare their country to the more developed states. The urban middle stratum began to feel the squeeze of economic and social immobilism, and the status of artisans continued to fall as foreign imports increased. Finally a small but determined labor movement began to knock resolutely on the doors of the closed system, demanding in. All of these elements were brought to a crisis by the combined effects of the depression and the Chaco War.

In analyzing the development of national movements, the case of Bolivia indicates that two important factors must be taken into account: the reactions of the status quo elite, and the scope and intensity of popular participation in national political conflict. In Bolivia between 1935 and 1952 the status quo elite adopted a stance which was both intransigent and incompetent. While they were able to block reformist efforts, they were not able to eliminate counter-groups or to alleviate the basic socioeconomic problems which contributed to the popular disenchantment. As a result, counter-elites, originally reformist, became more radical, and there was a steady increase in the scope and intensity of social conflict. In the course of its sixteen-year battle, the MNR was transformed from a reformist elite cabal into a reformist party and finally into an authentic national popular movement.

The MNR mirrored the contradictions that wrack Bolivian society. Despite its unique aspects, the MNR is an example of a relatively general sociopolitical reaction to common problems of blockage in underdeveloped societies. Its internal problems are similar in kind to those experienced by other national popular movements. Such movements suffer from two basic lines of conflict: (1) conflict between the situational needs of the elites' development aims and the consumption demands raised by supporters of the movement, and (2) conflict arising from the fact that as a cross-class alliance the movement incorporates groups with different interests and aims, reacting to different problems. In an environment of scarcity, these differences eventually result in clashes over the distribution of rewards and costs.

The case of Bolivia indicates that, aside from implacable environmental factors, what one can expect from a successful national popular movement depends on when and how it comes to power. The MNR came to power by means of a genuine popular insurrection, which swept aside the crumbling foundations of prerevolutionary Bolivia. When the power of the state collapsed, the revolution unexpectedly spilled into the agrarian sphere, and the capacity to use force coalesced at regional and segmental levels.

A revolutionary seizure of power complicates the already severe problems inherent in national movements in underdeveloped countries by raising the issue of the legitimacy of the new sociopolitical order and the new government. Varying ideological images, class interests, and regional pretensions come into conflict with contradictory political and economic needs. Once the MNR lost the ability to use force on behalf of its ideological model, the tension between conflicting consumption demands and investment needs in an environment of extreme scarcity took hold. Almost immediately the vicious circle of political and economic decline set in.

The attempt by Paz Estenssoro to obtain a state capitalist solution came to grief for a variety of reasons, some unique to the Bolivian situation, others indicative of the underdeveloped situation itself. In any event, what had once been a successful national popular movement ended in failure. At this point, one can say little more than that the factors which undermined the MNR continue in Bolivia and that, in any future solution, Bolivia's refurbished army and her peasant masses will play key roles.

Notes and References

1. See, for example, *Análisis y proyecciones, del desarrollo económico*, IV, *El desarrollo económico de Bolivia*, Mexico: United Nations, 1958 (hereafter cited as *Análisis y proyecciones*); and Harold Osborne, *Bolivia: A Land Divided*, New York: Oxford U. Press, 1964.

2. For an excellent discussion of these political patterns see Herbert Klein, "The Impact of the Chaco War on Bolivian Society," unpublished Ph.D. dissertation, U. of Chicago, 1963.

3. *Análisis y proyecciones*, pp. 7–15; this section includes a number of tables illustrating the points made in the text.

4. Gino Germani and Kalman Silvert, "Estructura social e intervención

militar en América latina," in Torcuato S. DiTella *et al., Argentina: Sociedad de masas,* Buenos Aires: Editorial Universitaria de Buenos Aires, 1965, pp. 272–84.

5. An important study of post-Chaco War economic problems will be found in the report of United Nations Assistance Mission to Bolivia, *The Keenlyside Report,* United Nations, 1951.

6. Merle Kling, "Toward a Theory of Power and Political Instability in Latin America," *Western Political Qtly.,* March 1956.

7. For an important account of the ferment in this generation and a statement of the nationalist position, see Augusto Céspedes, *El dictador suicida,* Santiago de Chile: Editorial Universitaria, 1956, pp. 81–96.

8. Important discussions of the labor movement appear in: Klein, *op. cit.;* Robert J. Alexander, *The Bolivian National Revolution,* New Brunswick, N.J.: Rutgers U. Press, 1958; Agustín Barcelli S., *Medio siglo de luchas sindicales revolucionarias en Bolivia,* La Paz, Bolivia: 1956.

9. Very important accounts of these two regimes are contained in two articles by Herbert Klein: "Davíd Toro and the Establishment of Military Socialism in Bolivia," *Hispanic American Historical Rev.,* February 1965, pp. 25–52; and "Germán Busch and the 'Era of Military Socialism'," *Hispanic American Historical Rev.,* May 1967, pp. 166–85.

10. The first official statement of the MNR appeared in a pamphlet entitled simply *Movimiento Nacionalista Revolucionario.* In Bolivia the pamphlet is commonly called *El libro verde.* A later MNR statement appears in Alberto Cornejo, *Programas políticos de Bolivia,* Cochabamba, Bolivia: Imprenta Universitaria, 1949 (hereafter cited as *Programas políticos*).

11. This statement should be qualified by noting that Víctor Paz Estenssoro and Walter Guevara Arze, both important party leaders, projected agrarian reform measures but these did not appear in the official party platform.

12. See Luís Peñaloza C., *Historia del Movimiento Nacionalista Revolucionario,* La Paz, Bolivia: Editorial Juventud, 1963, especially pp. 131–53.

13. Witness this statement by leaders of the then National Confederation of Labor: "En Bolivia como en todo el mundo, jamás los intelectuales han demonstrado sinceridad, afinidad y espíritu de lucha con las masas obreras, siempre llevan una intención oculta, un cálculo para traficar con nuestras fuerzas, siempre les guía el afán de encumbrarse a los cargos directivos, sin llegar antes a las bases, sin indentificarse con ellas, sin compenetrarse de sus dolores, angustia y rebeldías." Barcelli, *op. cit.,* p. 155.

14. A reprint of the thesis appears in *Programas políticos,* p. 314.

15. The distrust of the old guard MNR leadership for Lechín is clear in Peñaloza's history of the party, which, in a sense, is a party history from the old guard's point of view.

16. Reported in the La Paz daily, *El Diario*, November 7, 1951, p. 3.

17. The fear, on the part of some MNR leaders, of unleashing the *campesinos* is reported in Fellman Velarde, *Víctor Paz Estenssoro: El hombre y la revolución*, La Paz, Bolivia: 1955, p. 228.

18. The long course of the Bolivian inflation is illustrated in the following table, which gives the rate of growth in the cost-of-living index:

1936–39	50.74%
1940–43	23.74
1943–45	7.7
1945–51	18.28
1952–53	173.0
1953–54	99.6
1954–55	68.9
1955–56	196.4
1952–56	147.58%

Figures for 1956 are based on the rate of growth for July–October (17.34 percent per month). Source: *Análisis y proyecciones*, p. 62.

19. Since the last years of the Siles government, *campesino* militias have been used with increasing frequency to break mine strikes.

20. Important works on post-1952 economic problems are: *Análisis y proyecciones*; Cornelius Zondag, *The Bolivian Economy 1952–65*, New York: Praeger, 1966; David G. Green, "Revolution and the Rationalization of Reform in Bolivia," *Inter-American Economic Affairs*, Winter 1965, pp. 3–27; Carter Goodrich, *The Economic Transformation of Bolivia*, New York: School of Industrial and Labor Relations, Cornell U. Bulletin 34.

21. COMIBOL's problems are discussed in the above works and in an important 9-volume study, prepared in 1956 by the New York Engineering firm of Ford, Bacon, and Davis.

22. MNR relations with labor are well covered in Alexander, *op. cit.*, and in *Labor Law and Practice in Bolivia*, U.S. Department of Labor BLS Report No. 218.

23. See *Análisis y proyecciones*, pp. 19–20 and "Ideas preliminares para la elaboración de un diagnóstico de la economía boliviana," *Planeamiento*, La Paz, Bolivia, No. 1 (December 1960), pp. 68–69.

24. This point does not imply the need of authoritarian or totalitarian government but rather recognizes the minimal need of a national order embodied in a state, which, if it does not direct development, can at least provide an environment hospitable to it.

25. Quoted in Chalmers Johnson, *Revolutionary Change*, Boston: Little, Brown, 1966, p. 35.

26. Important studies of the agrarian situation in Bolivia are: Richard

Patch, "Bolivia: U.S. Assistance in a Revolutionary Setting," in Richard Adams *et al., Social Change in Latin America Today*, New York: Vintage, 1960; Dwight Heath, "Land Reform in Bolivia," *Inter American Economic Affairs*, Spring 1959; Barbara Léons, "Changing Patterns of Social Stratification in an Emergent Bolivian Community," unpublished Ph.D. dissertation, U.C.L.A., 1966.

27. Discussions of economic immobilism appear in the articles by Green (n. 20, above) and Patch (n. 26).

28. By 1957 one observer could note: "Los sindicatos podrían vivir sin el partido, pero es dudoso que el partido sobreviviría sin los sindicatos." Noel Pierre Lenoir, *Revolución: Altitud 4,000 Metros*, Buenos Aires: Editorial Cátedra Lisandro de la Torre, 1958, p. 97.

29. A review of any paper on the Bolivian situation will demonstrate that reported incidents of strikes, political murders, regional wars, and other forms of violence increased significantly after 1952.

30. Stated in his MNR speech, "La revolución es un proceso que tiene raíces en el pasado," La Paz, February 1961.

31. See the Ford, Bacon, and Davis report (n. 21, above). The Eder report was a private memo to the Bolivian government. Its major measures are listed in *Análisis y proyecciones*, pp. 80–82.

32. The growing negative attachment of the Left to the MNR is clear from the following statement of Lechín: "Aún concediendo que el régimen actual no interprete en un cien por ciento las grandes masas de la ciudad y del campo, hay que preguntarse si éstas encontrarán intérpretes más consecuentes y claros, por ejemplo, en la Falange e en el Partido Auténtico. Como la respuesta no puede ser sino negativa, tiene forzosamente que convenirse que el apoyo al Gobierno del MNR es la posición justa." From "Discurso inaugural del Secretario Ejecutivo de la Central Obrero Boliviana," La Paz, Bolivia: 1962, p. 31.

33. Actually, the Cochabamba Valley situation was more complex. It appears that Paz first sought to supplant Rojas with a young new leader, Julian Chávez. Failing in this, Paz later attempted to win over Rojas. Rojas supported Paz but he made it clear that he considered Siles the true leader of the MNR, and later his name was linked with the rising star of René Barrientos.

34. Helio Jaguaribe, *Desarrollo Económico y dessarrollo político*, Buenos Aires: Editorial Universitaria de Buenos Aires, 1964, p. 68.

35. *Ibid.*, pp. 82–83.

36. Guevara's defection in 1960 relieved some pressure, but the number of job-hungry cadres remained quite high.

37. Reported in *Presencia*, January 18, 1964, p. 5.

38. In a number of discussions between the writer and both pro- and anti-

Paz *MNRistas*, Paz's progressive loss of control over the party in his last three years of office was continually stressed.

39. Among the more obvious signs of deterioration were the open and never punished murder of a minister of peasant affairs, the murder of Salas' pro-Paz rival in a daylight gun battle in downtown La Paz, and the brief sequestration of the President himself in the Cochabamba Valley.

40. The most-up-to-date breakdown of data on the Bolivian economy is *Economic and Program Statistics*, No. 8, U.S. AID Bolivia, December, 1966.

41. Since 1964, troops have twice invaded the mines and smashed strikes. Throughout the country the old-line unions have been smashed and their leaders exiled.

42. See especially Torcuato DiTella, "Populism and Reform in Latin America," in Claudio Véliz, ed., *Obstacles to Change in Latin America*, New York: Oxford U. Press, 1965, pp. 47–74.

Index

A

Affluent Society, The (Galbraith), 66

Agency for International Development (A.I.D.), 124–26, 129

Agrarian reform, 193, 194, 200, 201–02, 208, 211

Agricultural employment, 24, 30–31

Agricultural workers, 8

Alba, Victor, 151

Alberdi, Juan Batista, 168

Alegría, Ciro, 165

Alliance for Progress, 14, 16, 110, 117–58, 163, 174, 216; achievements of, 128–50; economic achievement of, 133; economic evaluation of, 143; and education, 147; external resources of, 130; first five years of, 150; future of, 151; and GDP, 137–43; health, 147; historical antecedents of, 119–21; and housing, 146; implementation of, 123–28; and income distribution, 148; investments, 137; and land reform, 148; and private foreign investment, 106–13; and public finance, 140; savings of, 139; social achievements of, 145; social evaluation of, 149

Alliance Without Allies (Alba), 151

Altiplano, 211, 218, 222, 224

Aramayo Corporation, 182, 192

Arendt, Hannah, 178

Argentina: agricultural employment, 30; artisan employment, 38; assistance from U.S., 136; central government expenditures, revenues, and deficits, 141; and common market commission, 157; electrical energy production, 35; exports, growth of, 135; and foreign capital, 130–32; gross capital formation, 138; gross domestic product, 39, 134, 138, 139, 141; gross domestic saving, 139, 140; gross investment, 137, 138; heavy-handed regimes in, 170; industrial employment, 36, 38, 40; industrial production, 25, 26, 32, 34, 37; intellectuals in, 168, 169, 174; and land reform, 148; manual vs. nonmanual employment, 47; military junta in, 13; nonagricultural employment, 30; nonmanufacturing employment, 41; occupational structure, 30, 33; per capita income, growth of, 133; per capita net product, 27, 28; and self-help, 144; service occupation employment, 43; social security system, 149; urban population, 29

Armies, Latin American, 13

Assistance, from U.S., (*table*) 136

Asturias, Miguel Angel, 174

Avramovic study, 69–70

B

Barrientos Ortuño, René, 224

Batista, Fulgencio, 165